What Others Have Said

"**I found this book very helpful and useful in daily living for people of all ages. It is very well written and an easy read.** It has excellent exercises that are very easily used to understand what social anxiety is actually and what the difference is between that and being shy. I myself had social anxiety from a very young age. My parents were abusive and controlling, and they made my life very difficult. But as an adult I have given speeches to college students and other professionals in front of many people. **I just wish I could have this book during my teenage years.** What you learn here in the book is that it is very normal for you to be shy and anxiety can be useful for certain situations but not if it interferes your life. I hope you will read this book whether you are young or old it can help."

-Theodore Cotchan, Speaker, Life Coach

"**As a trauma therapist and mom of three, I am always on the lookout for books to help others grasp the effects of difficult experiences on our peripheral nervous system. I love that this book references neuroscience, childhood emotional neglect, and anxiety as being experienced as a physical energy occurring within the body.** It also explains a process of noticing and naming emotions. Many of my clients think that something's wrong with their mind when they're struggling with anxiousness. This book does a great job of breaking down the value of prioritizing management of the sensations around anxiety which is the opposite of what many of us have been taught about anxiety. Telling our kids to "try to not think about it," isn't useful. Try to not think about a brown dog barking in front of a purple house! Doesn't work. When we teach them experiential exercises to address anxiety, we're giving them superpower skills that will benefit them in personally and professionally will serve them in relationships and as they work to meet goals!"

- Amazon Customer

SOCIAL ANXIETY WORKBOOK FOR TEENS

10-Minute Activities and Tools to Reduce Stress, Conquer Fear, and Boost Social Confidence

Blooming Minds

Disclaimer:

Please note the information contained within this document is for educa-tional and entertainment purposes only. All effort has been made to present accurate, up-to-date, reliable, and complete information. No warranties of any kind are declared or implied.

Readers acknowledge that the author is not engaging in the rendering of legal, financial, medical, or professional advice. The content within this book is derived from various sources. Please consult a licensed professional before attempting any techniques outlined in this book.

By reading this document, the reader agrees that under no circumstances is the author responsible for any direct or indirect losses incurred as a result of the use of the information contained within this document, including, but not limited to, errors, omissions, or inaccuracies.

Legal Notice:

This book is copyright protected. This book is only for personal use. You cannot amend, distribute, sell, use, quote, or paraphrase any part, or the content within this book without the consent of the author or publisher.

TABLE OF CONTENTS

Foreword

I regularly work with teenagers whose social anxiety completely control's their lives. They are often frozen in fear and unable to understand themselves or why they feel and behave the way they do.

We all experience anxiety at some point in our lives. Anxiety very often helps us to do better. A bit of anxiety can make us more focused, speed up our reactions and give us instant energy. When anxiety becomes excessive, it can undermine our confidence. Social anxiety is more than feeling a bit anxious.

Social anxiety is a prolonged and overwhelming fear of social situations. It can leave us feeling disproportionately fearful of being judged. We can end up feeling anxious just thinking about these situations and then avoid them altogether.

In recent years, I have watched, with the rest of the world, the increase in anxiety in teens as a result of pressure from external influences like social media, an increasingly scary and threatening world with information immediately available to us, and high expectations and pressure to succeed from the adults in their lives. Today's teens need a larger and more complex set of skills and strategies to help them cope with their emotional distress.

I personally don't often set "homework" for my teen clients, as they get enough of that from their place of education. But what I love about this book is how you can dip in and out of it, with some exercises taking only 5 minutes. I recommend it as something to work alongside therapy, with my client completing exercises between sessions to help them better under-stand themselves. Many of the activities can be worked through with a therapist or on their own.

The book gives teens and their adults a good understanding of the social anxiety's ins and outs with relatable examples. The illustrations are eye-catching, and the activities are engag-ing. The information given is backed up by research.

Those of us who work with teens in distress know just how hard it is to get them the support that they need. This book is a welcome addition to the toolbox for support that can be used alone, with parents and caregivers, or in therapy.

Katherine Wilson,
BSc (Hons) Psy, MBACP Adults, Children, and Young Peoples Counsellor

INTRODUCTION

"You don't have to control your thoughts. You have to stop letting them control you."

– Dan Millman

Have you ever felt like talking to people wasn't your thing? Like you would mess up the moment you opened your mouth to speak, and the whole world would remember it?

If you recognize these feelings and are asking, "How did you know?" that's because I've been there and done that myself, and I've seen how some of my friends and family members have struggled.

I've always wanted to share my experience and knowledge on how I tackled social anxiety in a world that didn't even recognize it existed. So this, along with current science and evidence-based therapies, inspired the creation of Blooming Minds, and the Social Anxiety Workbook for Teens. Social Anxiety is a widespread issue that can be overcome, and you'll learn how in this book.

Some level of stress and anxiety in daily life, such as feeling stressed out by a class presentation, is normal and expected. But when anxiety causes strong physical symptoms or feelings of dread or interferes with your ability to participate or complete the presentation, or social fears stand in the way of reaching your goals, or even participating in normal social activities, these may be examples of when you can benefit from exercises and strategies outlined in this book.

Avoiding or running away from the social situations causing you trepidation can actually make it worse. This book will encourage you and provide you with approaches to deal with anxiety-inducing social situations as they happen, therefore lessening anxiety over time.

Getting nervous or panicked about how to handle people can be an unbearable feeling, which can bring out deeply held negative feelings that make it hard to progress. If you have tried to battle social anxiety on your own, you've likely experienced that it's not easy. Exhausting, I would say. At some point, we may wish we could just become invisible, because then we would feel at peace...

Are you ready to find out why social anxiety happens and how to handle it?

This workbook won't teach you how to avoid feelings of discomfort in your life entirely. Discomfort can even be vital in certain situations. This workbook will show you how to have power over your thoughts, which lead to emotions and behaviors. You do not have to let your fears keep you from reaching your true potential.

HOW TO USE THIS WORKBOOK

The Social Anxiety Workbook for Teens is a step-by-step guide divided into two parts, spread across ten chapters.

In Part 1, we will dive into understanding social anxiety and how to differentiate it from shyness and introversion.

Part 2 is a road map for overcoming social anxiety. It includes a toolbox with valuable supportive material and strategies combined with 5- to 10-minute quick-write activities, affirmations, checklists, and worksheets. They will help you understand social skills concepts and how to mitigate them in social settings. You will learn how to boost your social confidence, build a positive mindset and overcome your fears.

With these tools, you can work through the signs and physical symptoms you've experienced. They will help identify the risk factors that may be worsening your social anxiety.

Take it from me – be patient. Rome wasn't built in a day, so don't get upset that things aren't working out immediately. One brick at a time until you make yourself a strong foundation. Keep up the daily practice even if the progress is slow. Jot down notes in your phone or supportive journal to have something to refer to when you need it.

Remember, social anxiety shouldn't run your life, and you won't be anxious forever. Eventually, you'll be able to take back your life and be more capable of keeping your mindset positive. You'll be able to do the things you thought you'd never be able to.

Imagine yourself holding a presentation to a crowd and not feeling weird in public anymore. Please think of this workbook as a booster, as we all need a little help once in a while. Give yourself permission to believe in yourself now more than you ever have before. You got this!

To Parents and Guardians:

Before offering your teen this workbook, please know that it is intended for ages 14 and up. Whatever their age, please be there for them. Your support and understanding are so valuable.

Building awareness about ways to overcome social anxiety isn't necessarily a simple task for any parent. Watching your beloved teenager suffer from social anxiety can be painful, and you may even find yourself facing feelings of guilt. Remember the *"Repetitio est mater studiorum"* Latin Proverb. Repetition is the mother of all learning.

Why this workbook?

What makes this workbook unique is the valuable information gathered from personal experiences reflected in the book's stories inspired by teens in real life and trusted sources to help those reading achieve their goals of gaining new social skills and conquering their fears.

This workbook can be a stepping stone to coping with social anxiety, but you may find seeing a therapist in addition to or along with using this workbook to also be beneficial.

At Blooming Minds, we are ambitious and committed to providing easy-to-use and accessible information and daily activities for teenagers and their caregivers to help them succeed. All you need is right here within these pages.

PART 1:

UNDERSTANDING SOCIAL ANXIETY

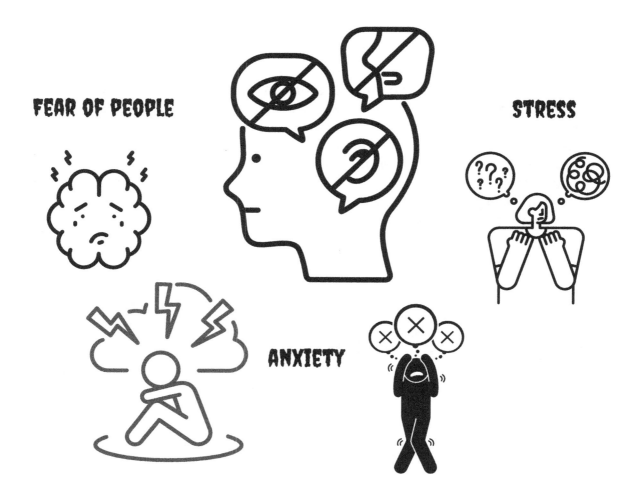

FEAR OF PEOPLE

STRESS

ANXIETY

Chapter 1

THE INS AND OUTS OF SOCIAL ANXIETY

"You cannot always control what goes on outside, but you can always control what goes on inside."

— Wayne Dyer

Until a couple of years ago, my friend Allison was struggling with her social life. She couldn't find a proper way to express herself. She felt like she had no control over her thoughts and behavior when she was around people. She thought everyone was monitoring her. Her thoughts were that people around her were judging her appearance, facial expressions when talking, or attitude. Looking at it from the outside, the possibility of every person looking for those flaws in her was not realistic. But in her mind, she couldn't help but feel they were.

Because of this, she suffered from a lot of stress and insecurity. She reached out for help and found out that she had Social Anxiety Disorder. It took her a long time before she learned how not to let these negative thoughts control her life.

One of the most significant lies anxiety makes you believe is that you're alone. The truth is, however, you're not. Many teens – and adults, for that matter – experience or struggle with social anxiety every day.

You may be asking, "How do I know if I have social anxiety, and aren't just introverted or shy? What's the difference?"

Well, here's a quick yes-or-no questionnaire.:

1. Do you find it hard to speak to strangers or adults in person or over the phone?

2. Does having a conversation with your peers sound like a complicated or dreaded task to you?

3. Does the prospect of performing or speaking to a crowd make you panic?

4. Are you avoiding parties or sleepovers because you feel you won't like them or fear what others will think of you?

5. Does eating in public, studying at the school library, or doing otherwise routine activities around others make you feel overly self-conscious?

If you answered yes to three or more questions, you most likely are experiencing social anxiety. Most likely, how you see yourself in the above situations couldn't be further from the truth.
You may feel like your heart wants to explode (it won't), or that you can't breathe (you won't die from social anxiety). It may seem like everyone else has their emotions under control except for you.

Let's revisit some old memories.

Answering these questions might be hard now, but think of it as a necessary evil to help you get better faster.

Q: Do you remember the last time you got nervous around people?

A:_____

Q: What caused you to get nervous?

A:_____

Q: Did it affect your daily performance, or did you notice a change in how you conducted yourself because of your anxiety?

A:_____

Q: Did it cause you to distance yourself from friends and family?

A:_____

Please keep these answers in mind, and refer to them when doing other activities in this workbook.
You have started elaborating on the discovery process, and that's the first big step in overcoming social anxiety.

Peter was a good kid, with straight A's, and always ready to do presentations in front of large groups. He was the student-of-the-year several times.
Some kids felt inferior around him, even though he was a very easy-going young man and always ready to help.

Rather than asking him for help, they ganged up on him after school one day. They beat him up and threatened that he would get beaten again if he told anyone. Scared, Peter kept his mouth shut.

He couldn't understand why they were being mean to him, because he never offended anyone.

He began having thoughts like, "What did I do wrong?" "Why am I treated like this?"

"Nobody should find out because they will think I'm a loser."

Unfortunately, the beating and bullying continued.

Even though he kept his mouth shut, they would take his lunch if he got an A on any assign-ment. Or give him the stink eye when he answered a question in class, and tear up his books.

After a while, Peter's behavior changed. His grades declined from straight A's to hardly getting a D.
He would freeze and start sweating and feeling uncomfortable when asked to answer a question or give a presentation.

Eventually, Peter stopped talking to his peers and spending time with them. All that to avoid problems of any sort from these bullies. He had developed a social phobia.

We know that anxiety is normal in certain situations. But look at how intensely Peter was experiencing it. He didn't know how to stick up for himself, nor did he tell a trusted adult like his parents or school counselor, about what happened. His ongoing fear of scrutiny and judgment had become social anxiety that was negatively affecting all areas of his life.

Social anxiety disorder, also sometimes referred to as social phobia, can cause you to withdraw from or avoid friends and loved ones. It can also cause you to focus on needing approval or validation from others more than is necessary.

SIGNS AND SYMPTOMS OF SOCIAL ANXIETY DISORDER

Signs are known reactions to an issue. And symptoms are what you're experiencing due to an unknown problem. So, let's review the known signs and symptoms of social anxiety and see which you can relate to.

Emotional and behavioral signs:

- Intense fear of social situations where negative judgment might be present.

- Fear or anxiety during a social event, with or without interaction.

- Constant fear of others' opinions in regard to you.

- Worries about showing physical symptoms, such as blushing, sweating, trembling, etc., while in front of a group.

- Avoidance of speaking in front of others, which leads to anxiety or panic.

- Spending a lot of time analyzing and critiquing past interactions with other people.

Physical symptoms. Powerful and unpleasant physical sensations often accompany social anxiety. You may feel you have no control over these symptoms, which can make your anxiety even worse. Physical symptoms of social anxiety include:

Faster heartbeat

Trembling

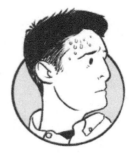

Sweating

Upset stomach &
nausea

Trouble catching
your breath

Hyperventilation &
panic attacks

Dizziness or
lightheadedness

Feel that your mind
has gone blank

Muscle tension

Avoidance symptoms. Regular or routine activities can seem complicated or impossible when social anxiety is present, and there is a tendency to avoid them. Let's review some of them:

- Attending parties and other social events.

- Initiating a conversation.

- Talking to strangers face to face or by phone.

- Making and holding eye contact.

- Walking into a room filled with seated strangers.

- Getting a refund for already purchased items in a store.

- Consuming food among other people.

- Making use of a lavatory in public.

We will elaborate more on this in upcoming chapters. For now, let's do a quick discovery interaction to find out where you lie on the social anxiety scale.

Rate with a number, using the key below, how you felt in the following social situations.

Key: 1 – Strongly disagree/Never.

2 – Disagree/Rarely.

3 – Sometimes/Somewhat.

4 - Agree/Often.

5 – Strongly agree/Very often.

1. Do you get anxious or feel a certain fear and self-consciousness when a crowd is watching you during a presentation?

1	2	3	4	5

2. How often does this happen when doing routine daily activities in the presence of others?

1	2	3	4	5

3. Would you agree that the fear you experience is unreasonable when considering the situation?

1	2	3	4	5

4. Do you actively avoid social situations that cause anxiety or find a way to remove yourself from them?

1	2	3	4	5

5. When you encounter social situations you have to endure, do you suffer intense uncomfortableness or other physical symptoms of anxiety?

1	2	3	4	5

6. Would you agree that social anxiety or avoidance of social anxiety-inducing situations affects your performance in school, work, and relationships with family and friends?

1	2	3	4	5

. How long you have felt this way?

1. For a few days.

. For a few weeks.

. For a few months.

. For a few years.

. More than a decade.

. Is the fear or anxiety you experience attributed to any substance (prescribed or illegal drugs) or a medical condition?

1	2	3	4	5

Scoring:

A score between 0 and 10 - low anxiety level.

A score between 20 to 30 - is an average anxiety level.

And a score between 30-40 - is a severe anxiety level.

Editor's note: *This assessment is not a medical tool, and it shouldn't take the place of a professional diagnosis. Use it simply to gather information. Only a qualified mental health expert or a doctor should diagnose mental health disorders. Regardless of the outcome of your assessment, we recommend discussing your results with a qualified mental health professional.*

THE DIFFERENCES AND SIMILARITIES BETWEEN SHYNESS/INTROVERSION AND SOCIAL ANXIETY

Statistics show that anxiety disorders are among the most common mental health issues in the United States.[1]

Being shy or introverted is often misinterpreted as having social anxiety. The table below highlights the differences between shyness and social anxiety, although the signs and symptoms may look the same.

SHYNESS	SOCIAL ANXIETY
1. Feeling uncomfortable in social situations.	1. Feeling afraid of social situations.
2. Feeling uncertain in new situations.	2. Feeling uncertain in all situations.
3. A personality trait that gets better over time.	3. A mental health disorder that gets worse over time.
4. Declines after the event.	4. Persists before, during, and after the event.

Common characteristics of shyness include:

• Being quiet or passive around others, also regarded as blending into the background

• Avoiding or limiting eye contact

---

[1]   About 40 million adults (19.1%) suffer from an anxiety illness. Meanwhile, 7% of children between 3 and 17 struggle with anxiety yearly, and symptoms often appear before age 21. The "Diagnostic and Statistical manual of Mental Disorders" (DSM-IV) defines social anxiety disorder as: - a condition that can cause everyday functioning issues that may persist for at least six months.

- Excessively rehearsing what you want to say

- Stammering

- Hesitance to try something new

Over time, social anxiety disorder symptoms, if not addressed, may worsen. Experiencing many life changes, stressors, or responsibilities can trigger more anxiety. Avoiding situations or people that make you anxious may make you feel better in the short term, but may cause bigger problems in the long term if you don't receive the proper support to address your social anxiety.

AS A PARENT OR GUARDIAN, HOW DO I KNOW IF MY TEEN IS STRUGGLING WITH SOCIAL ANXIETY?

You may wonder why your happy kid has started shying away from or avoiding social situations, school, or certain people. They may talk less about school or friends. Your teen may have a reduced appetite at mealtime, prefer to stay at home, or spend more time in their room than usual.

These all can be normal teen behaviors to some extent, or they can be signs of other concerns as well. More specifically, if you notice a change in social habits that is unexpected or more withdrawn or avoidant than usual, social anxiety may be a factor to consider or inquire about with your teen.

1. Talk to them. Let's be honest, this isn't easy. Teenagers don't like talking to their parents about "life issues." They don't want to be seen as "children," even though technically they are.

Teens tend to ignore you or push you away, not telling you about the issues they're having. Approach with empathy and compassion rather than accusations or diminishing their concerns. Please be open to them and willing to listen to anything your child says about their feelings. Share your concerns and tell them you're there for them – and then be there – without judgment or a lecture.

2. Set up a mental health consultation. There are qualified therapists and mental health professionals out there who can help. Find a good one and get your teen evaluated. Ask your pediatrician for a checkup to determine if any medical issues contribute to your teen's depression or anxiety. Keep your teen informed of the plans you're making every step of the way, and don't try to force them into doing anything.

3. Registering for therapy sessions. Some of you may believe this is irrelevant and say: "Why does my child need a therapist? or "Why does my child need to open up to someone else when they have me?" Trained mental health professionals go through years of schooling and are knowledgeable about the things you may be missing. Give them the chance to help you form a better relationship with your teen.

4. Learn as much about social anxiety as you can so you can offer better support. Learn everything you can about social anxiety. This workbook can be an excellent tool in your learning process. It covers a general overview of Social Anxiety Disorder, offering various methods and practices to mitigate it.

Learning about your kid's feelings and providing comfort and encouragement is very important. Your knowledge and support will give them a reason to put effort into getting better.
We will revisit and practice some of these steps again in the next chapter.

CAUSES OF SOCIAL ANXIETY DISORDER

There is no known single cause of social anxiety disorder. As with many other mental health conditions, it is most likely the consequence of several factors interacting with each other.

Any factor that can increase your chances of developing a disorder following a stressful event is known as diathesis. Diathesis, coming from the Greek word for "disposition," can present itself in many ways, either as a biological factor, traumatic experience, or even a situational circumstance. For example, imagine multiple cups, each filled with a different number of marbles. When pouring water in, the cups with more marbles will overflow quickly.

The diathesis[2] is similar to marbles, while stress is like water — the more substantial the diathesis, the less pressure requires to create "overflow" (i.e., give rise to mental health conditions).

---

2   According to the Diathesis-Stress Model, you have to have a diagnosis and a stress factor (which could be a person, thing, or set of hard life issues) to trigger the start of your mental health disorder. However, those with a substantially higher tendency to a disorder may need less pressure to be activated, and vice versa. It contributes to the "nature vs. nurture" debate in psychology – whether disorders are primarily produced by those underlying biological characteristics ("nature") or by social and environmental circumstances ("nurture") – by explaining how both can live together to generate a problem.

MAJOR CONTRIBUTORS TO SOCIAL ANXIETY

Inherited traits. If you have parents or grandparents with social anxiety disorder, there's a 30-40 percent greater chance of developing the condition yourself. You get genes from your parents responsible for boosting calmness and moods and inducing "fight-or-flight" responses.

Human brain structure. The amygdala, a part of your brain, is responsible for processing the emotion of fear. Social interactions or events that trigger fear can cause hyperactivity in the brain. As a result, the amygdala can't distinguish between an ordinary situation and an actual threat.

With modern methods like neuroimaging, medical specialists can examine different functions in specific brain regions based on the blood flow and brain anatomy. When you experience anxiety, four brain areas are activated. They are:

- The cerebral stem (controls your heart rate and breathing)

- The limbic system (affects your mood and anxiety level)

- The frontal lobe (helps you to assess risk and danger)

- The cerebral cortex (controls your muscles)

Environment. Social anxiety disorder may be a learned behavior influenced by:

- A traumatic experience such as bullying, the loss of a loved one, or prolonged or traumatic illness.

- Anxious parenting, controlling behavior, and overprotective approaches are linked with anxiety disorders and can affect a child's self-image and beliefs.

- There are cultural factors to social anxiety, such as differences in prev-alence, symptoms, and feared scenarios.

RISK FACTORS FOR SOCIAL ANXIETY

Several circumstances may increase the chances of developing a social anxiety disorder. They include:

- **Family history**. You are more prone to social anxiety disorder if your biological parents or siblings have it, too.

- **Negative experiences**. If you have been harassed, bullied, rejected, or humiliated in one way or another, you are more likely to have a social anxiety disorder. Also, other unpleasant life experiences, such as separation and divorce, trauma, or abuse, can be linked to the development of this condition.

- **Mood changes**. Are you shy, introverted, or restricted to an unhealthy level by your parents? It is highly possible that when you are confronting unfamiliar situations or people, you may be more vulnerable to social anxiety and trying to please people to show you're good enough.

- **New social or professional obligations**. Most symptoms of social anxiety disorder first appear during the teenage years. You get to meet more people and gain more responsibilities. Working a job can present more challenges and stressors, such as presenting in front of a group.

- **Differentiating characteristics**. For example, a facial irregularity, skin conditions, stuttering, or other differences from peers in background, speech, appearance, or abilities can heighten feelings of self consciousness and social anxiety.

So, we have established that social anxiety is a dread of interacting with others and dealing with social situations. You can recognize your own symptoms of social anxiety. Therapists and other mental health professionals can determine how serious it is and can work with you using various therapies to improve or eliminate your symptoms.

You've also read about the various signs and symptoms of social anxiety, and how to differentiate between shyness and social anxiety. Here's where you practice what you've learned.

Please pinpoint if Anna and Kennedy, from the two stories below respectively, are suffering from social anxiety or shyness. Let's see if you can identify the difference between the two examples and write down your answer.

Anna:_____

_____

Kennedy:_____

_____

Anna is a 15-year-old girl enrolled in a new high school after her family moved to a new town. She was always quiet and preferred to be by herself.

Her science assignment was to give a presentation in class. She had practiced for days, and when it finally came time to present, she decided she couldn't do it.

When the teacher called her name, Anna was very nervous, sweating profusely, and hyperventilating. The teacher took her to the school nurse, where Anna explained that she felt like throwing up and that the whole room had gone dark.

Kennedy *is also a 15-year-old girl enrolled in a new high school in the middle of the semester because her mom's job changed, and they had to move. At the new school, Kennedy felt very intimidated by her new classmates.*

In her biology class, Kennedy's assignment was to do a presentation. When she walked in front of the group, she felt all eyes were on her. Kennedy knew what to say and how to put it, even though she was nervous. The best way for her to give the presentation was not to look anybody in the eye. She said she felt overwhelmed but wasn't scared and wanted to hurry up and sit back down.

You probably were able to see the differences between Anna and Kennedy's stories. The difference between social anxiety disorder and shyness is the degree to which fear impacts the person's experience. A shy person can overcome their reluctance without panic, while a person with a social anxiety disorder may find it more difficult or impossible to work through or overcome the feeling of fear.

 5-minute exercise:
SOCIAL ANXIETY SYMPTOMS CHECKLIST

With the help of this checklist, you can grade the number of symptoms you have experienced or are experiencing now. Write down anything else that's not on the list. Show them to your doctor or therapist at your next visit.

SYMPTOMS	YES	NO
Irregular heartbeat or chest pounding		
Heart racing		
Dizziness		
Lump in throat		
Nausea or a sickening feeling in your belly		
Blurred vision		
Headaches		
Chills		
Tightness in your chest		
Shortness of breath		
Ringing in your ears		
Flushed cheeks		
Split personalities		
Derealization (feeling like you or your surroundings are not real)		

Shakiness or tremors		
Changes in your eating and sleeping patterns?		
Feelings of guilt or worthlessness		
Other symptoms (list below)		

15-minute exercise:
THE ORIGINS OF YOUR SOCIAL ANXIETY

Genetics: List the people in your extended biological family who have difficulty with any anxiety, including social anxiety. Include people who are "shy" or "quiet."

_____

_____

Family environment: What did you learn from your parent(s) or primary caregivers about handling new social or performance situations?

_____

_____

How much did your parents or caregivers encourage you to do things even if they made you nervous? What did that teach you?

_____

_____

Did your family strongly emphasize being concerned about other people's opinions (for example, did you hear, "Don't do that – what will the neighbors or family or friends think?" If so, what did you learn from this?

_____

_____

Did your parents or caregivers socialize or talk in front of groups such as work or community or religious groups? What did you learn from this?

_____

_____

Did you have a parent or caregiver who abused you emotionally, physically, or sexually? Did you have one who did not help you meet basic needs (physical care, emotional support)? If so, how did this affect how you view yourself and other people?

_____

_____

Essential experiences: Describe any harmful or traumatic social experiences you think might be significant in the development of your social anxiety. How did these experiences affect how you view yourself and other people?

_____

_____

Summing it up: Looking over the information in this last exercise, draw a pie chart dividing up how significant you think genetics, family environment, and essential experiences have been for you in the development of your social anxiety.

This activity aims to weigh the pros and cons of any decision you're about to make. Practice doesn't make perfect; you're human and can't be perfect. However, you can improve, and the more you think about the pros and cons of any decision you're about to make, the faster it becomes a habit until you don't need to write it down anymore.

	Decision	Pros	Cons
1	I am working on my social anxiety starting today.	One positive change this will bring is …	My fears about why it might not work out are...

2	I am staying the way I am, not changing anything.		
3	I am going to talk to my parents about my fears.		
4	I am going to see a therapist.		

Takeaway: We covered the most important points in understanding social anxiety, its origins, risk factors, and how we can identify it and differentiate it from shyness. In the next chapter, we will delve even deeper into the anxiety response and why our brains are hard-wired for fear in the first place.

Chapter 2

SOCIAL ANXIETY, THE BRAIN AND FEAR RESPONSES

By now, you know what social anxiety is and the risk factors that can make you more susceptible to social anxiety. You also know more about possible causes, signs, and symptoms. Now let's examine why we experience anxiety and how we can challenge it.

Most of the time, the most trivial of matters can cause significant stress, depending on the person. Our brains define stress based on the society we live in. Many generations ago, our ancestors

lived in an immediate-return environment, using stress and anxiety as a means to survive.

The immediate-return environment is an environment that deals with basic human needs and threats as they happen, such as:

•   You find shelter when you need to sleep.

•   You find food and water when you need to eat or drink

•   You run or hide when you see a

lion or menacing predator.

This was what every other animal did back then. Like deer, even the crack of a branch was enough to put them on high alert that there could be a threat to their survival. That anxiety helped humans stay alive, and everything returned to normal once the human or deer felt safe.

In the more recent past, as modern society formed and came to be what we know now, humans have the ability and time to think more about possible future problems. This can be thought of as a delayed-return environment.

This uncertainty about how to create solutions to solve future problems became a source of ongoing stress and anxiety. Here are a few examples: Reading a week ahead to pass a test next week, doing your assignments early in summer break, so you don't have to rush by the end of summer break.

The big question now is, why? Why do we stress over the future? Why can't we do it the old way? To answer that, let's check out the human brain and anxiety over the years.

THE HUMAN BRAIN AND ANXIETY

Think of the brain as a phone. Over the years, it has progressed from buttons to flip phones, smartphones with bigger screens (tablets and pads), and touch screens.

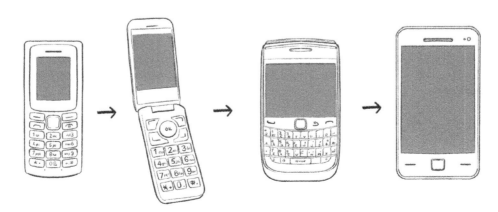

But it still retains its essential function: **communicating**. Your brain has changed tremendously from the time of your ancestors – the cavemen, whose only thoughts were to solve the next immediate problem or meet the next basic need. Then, the brain was well suited for handling those problems, but now, we live in a more developed world. And just like every other animal, we have tried to cope. With the creation of new things, comes the need to learn how to use them.

For example, let's say you want to build a Lego castle. To do that, you'll need Legos, and you'll need to know what a castle looks like and how to make it. So, you run around gathering information on building a castle from library books and online.

But for you to get Legos, your mom has asked that you ace your English test. Now you have to study and pass with an A+. But you're not so good at English, so you need a classmate or a teacher's help. You feel uncomfortable asking them.

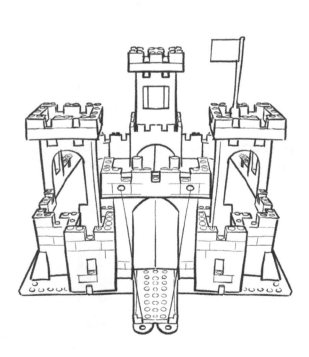

You are having thoughts like, "What will they think of me?" "They will say that I'm dumb." And that stresses you out even more. Now you are starting to collapse under pressure, and you ask yourself, "Is it worth it?" "How do I find a way to avoid their judgment and still pass English?"

The list goes on and can spiral for much longer. At first, stress and anxiety were beneficial because they alerted you to take care of immediate, short-term problems. It's amazing how long you've been able to cope with the increased stress levels in dealing with the problems of a delayed-return environment. Give yourself some credit.

HOW DO YOU COPE IN A DELAYED-RETURN ENVIRONMENT?

When you face stressors like, *"Will I be able to skate like Ryan?"* or *"Will I be able to make it as student of the year?"* It's like you are trying to solve problems with the immediate-return mindset in a delayed-return environment. Meanwhile, you haven't given it enough time to work out. But that's just a single response to the problem.

Someone else could work hard for the ability to skate like Ryan or be named student of the year, and someone else could completely shy away from this type of competition. This book aims to give you coping strategies to deal with social anxiety so you can face your problems and conquer your fears.

Measure your goals. Measuring your goals doesn't mean using a scale or mathematical formula. A good example would be studying for a test. If you can measure how many times you need to read in a week to get an A on your test, you have a better handle on the problem and what it will take to solve it, which can help reduce anxiety.

Redirect how you worry. This is about creating a routine to reduce anxiety. For example, instead of worrying about failing your tests, put that energy into creating and following a daily studying and homework routine. This strategy rewards you right away (immediate return) as well as solves your future problems (delayed return).

Think before you respond. A stress response is an emergency response to a perceived incoming threat. Your central nervous system is in charge of your response to stressful situations. In short-term cases, stress can be beneficial. If your stress levels stay high or longer than necessary, your brain will send signals to release stress hormones, which can impact your mental and physical health over time.

THREE RESPONSES TO ANXIETY

Being anxious is quite similar to being afraid, except that anxiety persists when there is no actual threat. Individuals experience some level of stress every day, but some people experience it more than others. Stress is a natural reaction to a perceived threat, and anything can cause stress, from discussions to recollections to tragedy and current events.

There are three main types of responses to threats, and these responses cause changes in the brain, allowing you to act as quickly as possible so you can protect yourself.

Fight response. This is an active defense mechanism that converts adrenaline into action, and you find yourself fighting to take control of the situation. For example, you'll get in trouble if you're getting bullied and start fighting back. But at that moment, there's a more significant threat in front of you, and you are trying to protect yourself.

Flight response. This is also an active defense mechanism that converts the same adrenaline into running away or escaping. You may experience symptoms similar to the fight response, including increased heart rate,reduced pain perception, and sharper hearing.

Freeze response. This is your body putting fight-or-flight on hold. It feels like your brain is booting up just like a computer boots up before actually taking action.

These are all unconscious mechanisms (automatic reactions) that can be worked on and managed.

Once a response has been triggered, changes occur in the body, and three significant systems are affected:

Physical system. Earlier, we established that adrenaline and other hormones are being emitted, but from where? Your autonomic nervous system! This system has two branches – the sympathetic and the parasympa-thetic branch.

The sympathetic branch is responsible for the activation of various parts of the body in response to the 3 Fs (fight, flight, or freeze).

The adrenal glands release the chemicals adrenaline and noradrenaline into the kidneys. They are messengers to maintain the physical changes for a considerable time or until the threat dies. Physical changes when the sympathetic branch is activated include:

- Increased heart rate

- Change in blood flow to larger organs and muscles, which can result in chills and numb or tingling body parts

- Increase in speed and depth of breath, which can lead to hyper-

ventilation or breathlessness

- Increase in sweating

- Widening of the pupils

- Decreased activity in the digestive system

- Muscle tension

Once a perceived threat has passed, the body returns to a more relaxed state. The autonomic nervous system once more controls this, but this time it gives the parasympathetic branch instructions to stop the process of either running away or standing and fighting.

As a result, the heart rate begins to slow, the breathing slows, the body's temperature begins to lower, and the muscles start to relax. The fact that the systems do not instantly return to normal is a part of the restoration process.

There is still some arousal, and for good reason. In the past, it would be risky to let our guard down too quickly and become unprepared when a wild animal approached us. The body continues to be ready for danger since there is a risk that it may occur in this situation. As a result, fight, flight, or freeze responses can take time to gradually fade. This makes it easier to see why some people experience anxiety for extended periods of time.

Cognitive system. When your brain is alerted to a perceived threat, the cognitive system focuses on shifting your attention to find where the threat is coming from, and you may find yourself actively searching for a danger that isn't there. When you can't find a physical threat, sometimes you can't accept that there's no reason to be frightened. You may feel like you're losing touch with reality.

Behavioral system. As you know, there are three behaviors or responses associated with anxiety, and when they are triggered, you might feel the urge to become aggressive, run away, or even freeze up. Most of the time, this isn't possible because you're in a social setting, so you express those urges by chewing your nails, constantly looking around for an exit, randomly tapping your feet, or even snapping at people because you're not comfortable.

PARENTAL SUPPORT: THINGS TO AVOID

In showing support for your teen with social anxiety, there are some things you should avoid, such as:

- **Criticizing**. Criticizing your child's attitudes or actions won't help them change their ways. Always emphasize positive progress.

- **Calling them shy**. When a parent, school counselor, or doctor describes a teenager as "shy," the teenager may believe that change is impossible. Labeling your teen could motivate them to use harmful coping mechanisms, particularly avoidance.

- **Blaming**. Don't hold yourself or your adolescent responsible for social anxiety. There are numerous potential initiating causes for the emergence of these symptoms. Think about the future and put change-making strategies into practice.

- **Allowing for avoidance**. Allowing your youngster to skip school or stay away from all social occasions will feed their anxieties. Encourage involvement while providing reasonable assistance and direction.

PARENTAL SUPPORT: THINGS TO DO

- Go over the anxiety's evolutionary roots.

- Learn more by talking with your teen about their particular difficulties.

- Help your teen to face their fears.

- Offer your support and discuss a potential visit to a therapist.

- Adopt a growth mindset to challenge negative thinking.

- Encourage your teen to implement calming techniques and try some calming techniques with them.

THE ROOT CAUSE OF SOCIAL ANXIETY

Fear is known as the root cause of social anxiety, but it is not a fear of "what is" but of "what isn't." This fear of judgment, embarrassment, and constantly thinking something is wrong with you contributes to the anxiety that social situations trigger. You can heal from these fears by:

1. Identifying the fears and ensuring they are not rooted in judgment or criticism.

	YES	NO
Do you believe that your opinions of others are flawed?		
Do you think it's wrong for people to judge you?		
Do you believe there is something wrong with your appearance or who you are?		
Are your fears of feeling inadequate and being judged realistic?		

2. Being aware of the root cause of social anxiety.

Many social anxiety cases begin with the fear of judgment and potential criticism from peers, parents, or strangers. Growing up, you might have been compared to your peers in one way or the other, either by appearance, performance, or behavior.

You've probably heard something like, *"Why aren't you top of the class like Stacey?"* or *"Stacey is prettier than you,"* or *"Why can't you be quiet like Stacey?"* This might make you begin to self-censor your actions so you can be like Stacey, and soon, you get uncomfortable with being yourself or being around Stacey.

At some point in your life, you've probably judged yourself based on negative criticism. If you think you'll never be like Stacey, you will most likely feel a sense of shame and inadequacy. Unfortunately, the more you allow yourself to believe that social anxiety is why you're afraid, the more you reinforce it.

You'll have to learn to see past your fears to realize that even if you or anyone else has a negative thought about you, it doesn't define you. That's just your fear talking.

3. Facing your fears.

To heal, you must be willing to face your fears and embrace who you are. Your worry will persist if you begin to think that social anxiety is something you should be scared of. Instead, work on accepting who you truly are. Free yourself from stereotypes or self-limiting assumptions, and believe that you can overcome this condition.

It's not about altering who you are to please others; it's about changing your mindset to reduce your concern over what others think of you. You must become your own best friend in order to use your strength and confidence for yourself rather than against yourself.

I am here to hold your hand and be by your side as you learn to see yourself in a positive light and accept and love this person more than anyone else. You are unique, and only you can contribute your unique gifts to the world.

TOOLS TO COPE WITH SOCIAL ANXIETY

A parent can help in numerous ways if their teen starts to show symptoms of social anxiety. Contrary to what some may believe, shyness, or feeling uncomfortable and apprehensive around new people, is not the same as social anxiety.

Although there are many ways you can manage your own anxiety and discomfort, you don't have to tackle it alone. Seeking help from a therapist or other qualified mental health professional is always a good idea. Some strategies used to treat social anxiety include:

Psychotherapy. A crucial component of the treatment plan used by most specialists because medication is only one piece of the puzzle in treating social anxiety and other mental health conditions.

With the help of psychotherapy, you can develop the social skills necessary to make significant changes while exploring your symptoms, emotions, and feelings in a safe environment. You can learn new strategies for coping through psychotherapy.

Cognitive Behavioral Therapy (CBT). One of the most common mental health treatments, CBT focuses on identifying and changing the negative thinking that affects your actions. You can learn to feel more in control and less apprehensive in social situations using cognitive techniques.

Negative automatic thoughts that contradict reality happen to people who might suffer from social anxiety. Because there are so many different treatments, choosing a therapist who knows the most successful techniques for treating social anxiety is critical. We will discuss and practice CBT in upcom-ing chapters.

Growth mindset. Mindsets may develop through communication with others such as friends, parents, and teachers, just like any other belief system. Encouragement to persist even when it gets tough is part of having a healthy growth mindset. It can apply to any goal you have, from talking to someone new to attending functions in crowded areas, leading presentations, or anything you find challenging but still something that you want to achieve. (Follow the chart below.)

For a growth mindset, "developing your passion" might replace "finding your passion." The first statement implies that interests and talents can be developed with commitment and perseverance, rather than being an inherent gift you either have or not, with no room for improvement or change.

Calming techniques. Calming techniques can be extremely effective in stress and anxiety management. Learning calming techniques can help, no matter how severe your social anxiety is. These techniques can be used anywhere, they are free or inexpensive, and they carry minimal danger. Calming techniques include:

Breathing. The act of breathing is so natural. There are techniques for mindful breathing that can quickly soothe our bodies and brains that we will practice in Chapter 8, Mastering Mindfulness.

Counting. Your mood can improve dramatically just by diverting your attention for a little while. Close your eyes and gently count to 10. It indeed does work! Once you reach the number you are counting up to, if you need more time, count to 20 or backward from 20.

Phone conversation. Call a friend – preferably a hilarious one. If that's not possible, call your parents or siblings. Making contact with a loved one can instantly calm you down. Endorphins, known as the "feel-good chemicals,", are released by laughter and have been shown to relieve stress and improve mood.

Aromatherapy. Take a lavender bubble bath or light a lavender candle. Lavender, chamomile, rose, and other stress-relieving essential oils are aromatherapy stars for anxiety relief.

Movement. Any form of physical activity aids in stress relief, such as yoga, massage, walking, biking, running, swimming, etc.

Work on your spirit and intellect. Do meditation, journaling, reading, cooking or baking, video gaming, or napping (in case you lack a night's sleep), just to name a few. Discover easy, relaxing methods that work for you reduce stress and enhance your general well-being.

DISCUSSING MENTAL HEALTH

As a parent, it is easy to assume what a teen's life is like. However, there is a lot of pressure they face on a daily basis. The COVID-19 pandemic and resulting global lockdown drastically affected teenagers, along with everyone else, all over the world. The statistics show increased mental health conditions during the height of the pandemic. But how can parents recognize and understand that their teen is struggling?

Instead of minimizing your teen's feelings or being dismissive by saying, "You are just shy or too emotional" or "Don't be so dramatic, it will go away," listen to them, hear them out.

Below are a few exercises that will benefit both teens and their parents or guardians.

10-minute exercise:
OPEN UP – for teens and parents

As a parent or a teen, how do you get each other to open up?

You'll need to start opening up and not waiting for the other person to open up first, and it's OK if you don't know how to start. You can use the following chart as a guide.

In the chart, answer the questions about specific challenges you've recently experienced.:

What's your most feared situation?	
Has anything traumatized you lately?	
Are you afraid of getting embarrassed?	
Do you feel introducing yourself will result in you being criticized or teased?	
Are you worried about what your peers think of you?	
How does that worry affect you?	
Do you hate talking in large groups?	
What experiences do you label as a failure?	
What do you think would happen if you did things differently?	
What is your worst possible result?	

As a parent or guardian, adjust your expectations when you speak with your teen and bring awareness to the fact that sometimes it is OK to make mistakes. They are a part of the growth process. Make mistakes, learn, and move on with your life.

10-minute exercise:
CONQUERING NEGATIVE THOUGHTS – for teens and parents

Conquering negative thoughts isn't an easy task. Teenagers can internalize and believe these negative thoughts and comments without much evidence to support them. Thoughts like, *"I'm inadequate," "I'm sure I will fail,"* and the like.

Complete this activity with your teen until they can do it themselves.

Write down 10 negative thoughts you believe about yourself.	Write down 10 negative thoughts you feel the general public has about you.	Come up with 10 positive explanations for these thoughts.

Letting your kid know that you also get nervous in social situations is an excellent way to let them understand that they are not alone. Explain to them what caused your nervousness and how you overcame it.

This might be a calming technique because, by consciously o ati these bodily responses, you've signaled to your brain that the panic you're in is unnecessary as there is no impending threat. Be honest about your emotions before, during, and after the event and how you overcome your fears. Please keep in mind that teens pick up a lot from observation.

Talking with your parents or caregivers about your worries might be challenging. But you can make the talk easier with a little preparation. Keep in mind that asking for help is OK. It might be a considerable comfort to express your feelings to someone! Reach out to your school counselor, a therapist, or another trusted adult if you don't feel comfortable approaching your parents.

Prepare your speech in advance by writing it down. Concentrate on communicating your current state of mind. You might say, *"I haven't been hanging out with my friends because I've been feeling down,"* or *"I have been finding it difficult to take part in class because I have been feeling apprehensive."*

Anticipate their possible reactions.

- If they respond that what you're saying seems typical, you could say, *"This is more than just a lousy mood. I am unable to handle this on my own."*

- If they make you feel bad about how you're feeling, you can say, *"I don't want to feel this way, which is why I think I need some more support."*

- If your parents believe they are to blame for your current problems, give them time to think things over.

- Enlist the help of someone else. Be it a friend, member of your family, or health care provider to assist you in having the conversation with your parent or guardian. Even the most devoted parents could initially respond with astonishment, defensiveness, or denial.

Consider communicating with your parents indirectly. If you're particularly anxious about opening up to your parents, consider writing a letter, email, or text to start the conversation.

Choose a suitable time and location.

- Most people find chatting with their parents or teens in the car more comfortable. If that is not true for you, try to choose a location where you're most likely to have your parents' undivided attention. It could be at home on a Sunday afternoon, on a car ride, or on a walk.

- Attempt to pick a time when you and your parents are all at ease and willing to talk.

Tell your parents how they can help. Your parents or caregivers might not know how to help because they don't know the details. Your job is to make them familiar with your feelings and symptoms. Think of ways they can assist you, such as scheduling a visit to a specialist. It can be the school counselor, a psychologist or therapist, or even your pediatrician or primary care provider.

One of the easiest ways to convey your thoughts is by writing them down. You can do letter writing, journaling, or even writing down notes for your conversations to keep you focused. **For example:**

To:
Mommy and Daddy

Dear Mom and Dad,

It hasn't been easy living like this for the past six months, not being able to tell you both what the problem was. I tried so many times, but there's no right way to it.

Dad, I can't keep doing this. I like playing basketball, but not at the competitive level. I want to play it because it is fun and not just because you want me to carry on the family's legacy.

Mom, I love you, but it has to stop. You both can't keep living your lives through me. Becoming a doctor is not what I want – I don't even know what I want to be. Because I've never had a choice, I want to find out for myself.

Every day I've tried to please you both. I go to all the basketball training, try and keep my grades up, and yet, I'm still the reason you fight all the time. Most of the time, I creep around the house, terrified that if either of you so much as hears me, it'll spark another fight, or that dad will ask why I'm not at practice, or mom will ask why I'm not studying.

I can't think properly. I can't breathe normally because it feels like the air stops when either of you enters the room. I haven't slept well in weeks because I keep having nightmares. The thought of you both in the same room makes me panic because I know there will be another fight or another criti-cism of how I'm living my life.

So please, I'd like you both to stop. Sorry if I'm disappointing you both. But I'm not okay. I need help, and you're not helping. If you want to help, please change my school. Kids are starting to bully me.

Did you know all the kids at school hate me and constantly remind me that I'll never measure up to Dad or Granddad? Mom, have you ever thought there is a different academic path for me and that the way you'd like me to take it isn't for me?

I want to tell you what I'm interested in and how you can help if you're willing to hear me out.

Love, Michael

Takeaway: To find the most successful coping strategies for yourself, you need to understand why they're effective. In the next chapter, learn more about the cognitive-behavioral model of psychotherapy and how it works with social anxiety.

Chapter 3

THE ESSENTIAL TRIO: THOUGHTS, FEELINGS, AND BEHAVIORS

Let's start off with a story.

Michael McKellen comes from a family of basketball players who all represented his school in the inter-state Michigan basketball competition. So naturally, his father expected him to carry out the family legacy. His mom, however, wanted him to become a doctor. Yes, that's right! It's our Michael, whose letter you just read.

Both his parents had different plans for his life, and he wanted to make them happy, but somehow, even that wasn't working out. The only way to maintain peace and stop all the arguing was to study hard and play hard.

Mike comes from a famous basketball family, and his life was already too complicated. He didn't have friends because he would spend all his time practicing. At school, the teacher assigned a few top students to help him study and boost his grades.

*He got bullied a lot. And because of that, he had all sorts of mean thoughts about himself such as, **"I'm only a basketball player because I'm a McKellen." "I am not that good; I am a disappointment to the McKellen family." "I'm a loser for associating with nerds."***

He'd often end up in fights with these bullies, and whenever his mom came to pick him up, he'd chalk his mood up to basketball practice because he didn't want to stress her out more than she already was.

"She is working two jobs and taking care of my disabled dad. This is already too much for her. I'm not going to bother her with my problems," *were some of the thoughts running through his head. One day after school, he suddenly heard yelling. He knew his parents were arguing about him.*

"They are fighting again because of me." "I'm the worst." *Michael felt ashamed and hurt. His mom didn't want him to play basketball again because he could get injured. His father said he'd be a disgrace to the McKellen name and his mom said he'd be a disgrace to the McKellen name if he didn't get his grades up. Michael was frozen in place, hyperventilating, breaking out in a sweat and chills as he trembled listening to his parents argue. When his parents finally took notice of him, it was far too late, and he bolted out the door to escape the fighting.*

Let's have a quick chat here.

- How do you think Michael's situation affected his mental health?

- Did Michael show any signs of stress or anxiety?

- Where did his problems start?

Yes, that is correct. None of these questions have a positive answer.

5-minute exercise:
THE ESSENTIAL TRIO

Now please identify the essential trio: Thoughts, feelings, and behaviors Michael experienced, following the first example:

Thoughts	Feelings	Behaviors
Micheal has negative beliefs about himself such as ...	Hyperventilating ...	To avoid disappointing his parents he ...

Your reactions to specific events, moreso than the events themselves, can make things difficult for you as a teenager.

The thoughts and feelings you have about something that happened affects how you handle yourself in that moment. Simply put, you can't control other people or situations that arise, you can only control yourself and your reactions to them. That's what the CBT model will help you do.

COGNITIVE BEHAVIORAL THERAPY (CBT)

Living your daily life, you tend to form your beliefs about yourself and others, and that affects your perception of the world and your behavior in it. A therapist can help you address these concerns. Please read the full definition of CBT in the corresponding footnote.[3]

Many situations in life and people's reactions are out of your control. How you react to them is where your power lies. Not every emotion you've felt is logical, nor is every thought you've had about yourself, and they can affect your behavior. Let's look at the example below.

---

3   CBT is a short-term psychological treatment practiced worldwide by numerous therapists. It is convenient and flexible, and it has been proven in its effectiveness in different formats such as face-to-face, online, and self-help books. That's why mental issues such as anxiety (including generalized anxiety disorder, panic attacks, social anxiety disorder), depression, obsessive compulsive disorder (OCD), post-traumatic stress disorder (PTSD), phobias, low self-esteem, etc., have been greatly improved in many cases over the past two decades by using CBT. Find a Certified CBT Therapist. (n.d.). Academy of Cognitive and Behavioral Therapy. https://www.academyofct.org/search/custom.asp?id=4410

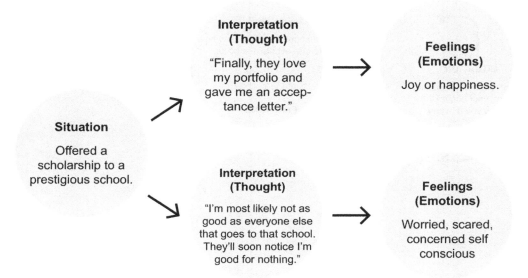

Situation

Offered a scholarship to a prestigious school.

Interpretation (Thought)

"Finally, they love my portfolio and gave me an acceptance letter."

Feelings (Emotions)

Joy or happiness.

Interpretation (Thought)

"I'm most likely not as good as everyone else that goes to that school. They'll soon notice I'm good for nothing."

Feelings (Emotions)

Worried, scared, concerned self conscious

How you react to a situation can have an effect on that situation. Here you might be asking whether CBT is right for you. The outcome of CBT is based on the level of effort and dedication you put in to practicing the skills you learn. As you use your CBT skills more, they will become a normal reaction to future events.

As for how long it takes to make CBT skills a part of your life, it depends on the severity of your social anxiety and how long you've dealt with it. If you haven't been experiencing social anxiety for very long, you will most likely overcome it more easily.

If your social anxiety is a long-time problem, say for a decade or more, give yourself more time to implement the CBT strategies you learn. A therapist trained in CBT can customize your treatment plan and share techniques that would be most beneficial in your individual case.

Regardless of whether you are a teenager or an adult, you can benefit from this workbook's activities and self-help techniques. With consistent effort, you will start to see results.

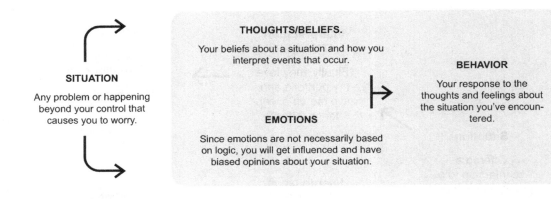

SITUATION
Any problem or happening beyond your control that causes you to worry.

THOUGHTS/BELIEFS.
Your beliefs about a situation and how you interpret events that occur.

EMOTIONS
Since emotions are not necessarily based on logic, you will get influenced and have biased opinions about your situation.

BEHAVIOR
Your response to the thoughts and feelings about the situation you've encountered.

THREE-COMPONENT MODEL OF EMOTIONS

To simplify the understanding of emotional change processes, CBT identifies a three-component model consisting of thoughts, feelings, and behaviors.

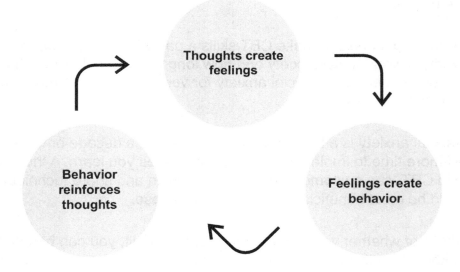

Thoughts create feelings

Feelings create behavior

Behavior reinforces thoughts

1. Thoughts. The way we interpret events can be referred to as thoughts. Thoughts can manifest in various ways, like verbally expressed forms like words, phrases, and concepts, and non-verbal forms like mental imagery. We constantly hear these thoughts in our heads as we go about our daily lives.

2. Feelings. Here, "feelings" refers to the physiological alterations brought on by an emotion. For instance, when we experience the emotion of rage, we may get a flushing sensation on our faces. We share the feelings of our heart racing and muscles tensing when we experience the emotion of anxiety. The physical representation of an emotion is called a feeling.

3. Behaviors. Simply put, behaviors are the actions we do or choose not to do. For instance, we could decline a speaking engagement if we have social anxiety. However, we could actively seek out such opportunities if we feel confident in our public speaking abilities.

These three elements shown in the illustration above interact with one another all the time, creating an emotional pattern and mood. If we are to modify one component, we will result in a chain reaction that will affect the other two. Taking Michael's story into consideration, when he came home and heard his parents arguing again, we would break down his situation like this:

- Thoughts: "They are fighting again because of me." "I'm the worst."

- Feelings: Ashamed and hurt.

- Behaviors: Bolted out the door.

SITUATION

Left the back door open in a rush to go play with friends and dog ran in and poop all over

THOUGHTS

Someone could have ransacked the house. I screw up everything. My parents are going to be so angry when if they find out. What a disaster!

THOUGHTS

Anxiety: face flushed, tightness in my chest, difficulty breathing
Shame: pit in my stomach
Fear and panic attacks

BEHAVIOR

Tried cleaning up, spent half the time panicking thus wasting more time. Made a bigger mess than before.

So first of all, Michael had automatic negative thoughts about himself, then he had negative feelings, and eventually, his thoughts and feelings influenced his behavior – escaping the scene.

 10-minute exercise: THREE-COMPONENTS OF EMOTIONS
Choose a situation that triggers a difficult emotion and identify the components of that emotion. See the example on the previous page and fill out the second diagram.

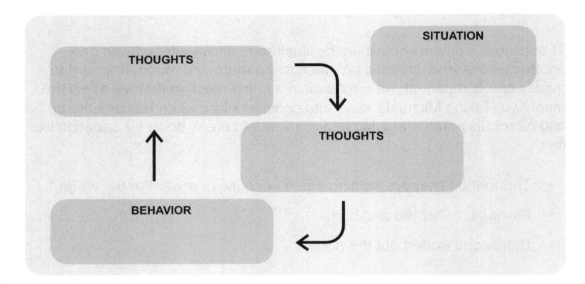

Alternatively, fill out this chart to help narrow down your thoughts, and write down your beliefs around that situation.

1. SITUATION (Try your best to describe the anxiety-provoking situation you had or are having.):

_____
_____
_____
_____
_____

2. THOUGHTS (Try your best to describe your thoughts during the situation.):

_____
_____
_____
_____
_____

3. EMOTIONS YOU FEEL AS YOU THINK ABOUT THOSE THOUGHTS (Check all that apply.):

☐ nervous   ☐ angry   ☐ irritated   ☐ hateful   ☐ sad

☐ frustrated   ☐ ashamed   ☐ embarrassed   ☐ other

4.   BELIEFS ABOUT MYSELF OR OTHERS:

_____
_____
_____
_____
_____

Editor's note: *Every exercise in this workbook is intended to teach you about fundamental mental processes so that you can feel better and accomplish your goals.*

The good news is that you can make your thought patterns work for you instead of against you. If you have social anxiety, small adjustments in your thoughts or behaviors can lead to a lessening of your symptoms. As you keep practicing these changes to your thoughts and actions, you will have more control over your feelings, and you'll feel more comfortable in the social situations you used to fear.

Making minor modifications in behavior and cognitive patterns in order to produce significant changes in feelings is what CBT helps people accomplish. Understanding this emotional mindset can improve the way you ap-proach issues and show you fresh approaches that will bring about positive changes in your life.

IDENTIFYING EMOTIONS

Most people aren't used to telling the difference between ideas and emotions. Addressing your feelings is made more challenging by the constant interchange of the two terms "feel" and "think" in the English language. We regularly use "I feel" and, "I think" somewhat interchangeably.

How frequently have you, for instance, heard someone say, "I feel like you're not listening to me," or "I feel like I did badly on the essay"? Actually, those are thoughts, not feelings. Compare those sentences to the emotional expressions "I feel excited," or "I feel scared." Each emotion may be summed up in a single word, but the five primary kinds of emotions are:

| Fear | Anger | Joy | Sorrow | Disgust |

In the table below, circle with a pencil the emotions that you are experiencing most often in your daily life.

Angry	Frustrated	Peaceful
Amazed	Foolish	Overwhelmed
Annoyed	Furious	Grievous
Anxious	Ashamed	Inadequate
Comfortable	Self-conscious	Insecure
Shocked	Depressed	Silly
Suspicious	Determined	Disdain
Content	Resentful	Hopeful
Worried	Nervous	Loving
Jealous	Irritated	Envious

Sad	Bored	Satisfied
Proud	Happy	Lost
Bitter	Stupid	Eager
Motivated	Joy	Hurt
Tense	Lonely	Terrified
Excited	Inspired	Miserable
Disgusted	Relieved	Uncomfortable
Confused	Embarrassed	Scared
Trapped	Worthless	Energetic

From the list of the emotions that your circled, chose five that you want to feel less. Every time you encounter these emotions, get curious about what is causing that emotion, and try to change your perspective on the people or situations connected to these emotions.

Why Do We Have Emotions?

If unpleasant emotions cause you so much grief, why do they even exist? It's typical to want to lessen or completely avoid some of these unpleasant feelings. At some point or another, it's all you've ever wanted. But ignoring or getting rid of emotional suffering is not ideal. Aside from the fact that suppressing or running away from emotions is not a realistic strategy (as you will discover later in this workbook), emotions – even the most painful ones – serve useful functions.

They serve as signals to ourselves. Emotions might drive you to act without waiting for a moment to think – in some cases, even before that. For instance, fear might indicate potential danger. Anger would drive you to protect your friends if someone attempted to harm them. In another example, you could decide not to consume spoiled food out of disgust.

However, since emotions are unreliable, they might not always indicate a genuine need for action. On thrill rides, when watching terrifying movies, or when startled by loud noises, you will have felt terror in the absence of danger. Emotional cues to act should not be taken as facts because of this; rather, they can be used as a source of knowledge.

They serve as signals to others. Emotions let people know how you're feeling and how they should react. Your facial expressions, posture, gestures, and other body language cues will communicate your feelings to others even while you are silent. If a friend witnesses you sobbing, they will assume that you are sad and feel moved to provide a shoulder to cry on. If a kid observes that you are terrified of snakes, he will learn that snakes are harmful and avoid them in the future.

LEARNING TO MONITOR YOUR MOODS AND EMOTIONS

Although emotions are essential and have useful purposes, they may sometimes overpower us and be toxic. To reach your goals, you can learn from this workbook how to connect to emotions in a different way.

Tracking and observing your emotional experiences is the first stage. Spend some time each day for the coming week thinking about the emotions you're experiencing by writing them down on the worksheet that follows.

You may either plan a certain time each day, such as just after dinner, to reflect on and write down the emotions you had, or you can do it whenever it strikes throughout the day. It could be helpful to set an alarm on your phone to remind you if you decide to record your emotions at around the same time each day.

Complete the following form to track your emotions each day, following the first example in the grid. Print out as many pages as you need.

1. Mark the date the emotion occurred.

2. Briefly describe the situation you were in when the emotion happened.

3. Identify the emotion(s) you felt and the intensity of each emotion on a scale from 1-10.

4. Identify the physical sensations associated with the emotion(s).

DATE	SITUATION	EMOTIONS AND INTENSITY	PHYSICAL SENSATIONS
09/07	Woke up late for school	worry(5), panic(7), shame(5), anger(6)	Racing heartbeat, the tension in my chest, neck, dizziness, feeling of heaviness

This exercise will help you identify your emotions, get curious about them, and reframe them until it becomes a habit, replacing negative emotions with a more positive mindset.

Takeaway: It's clear that thoughts, feelings, and behaviors all play an important role in social anxiety. In the next chapter, we're going to continue exploring the power of your thoughts and discuss how to identify maladaptive thinking.

Chapter 4

IDENTIFYING PATTERNS OF THINKING

"Your beliefs create your thoughts, which create your feelings and emotions, which cause the circumstances of your life."

– Awakening, By Dr. Erin Fall Haskell

Did you know that our minds love to lie to us and tend to convince us that circumstances result from our emotions?

That's right! It does that without us realizing that things are not as they appear. But here is the thing, it's not the outside circumstances that make us sad or anxious. It's how we interpret them; it's how we think about them. So, for example, you might think, *"I'm upset because I didn't get an A on my math test."* And your brain goes, *"Oh, I am such a failure."* Instead of thinking, *"Oh, I didn't prepare enough last night because I was playing video games."* Or you might think, *"Nothing good ever happens to me,"* instead of *"I will try to be more prepared for the next test."*

Your thoughts shape your world, and it's no wonder that falling into the trap of negative thinking can have severe consequences on life satisfaction, relationships, and feelings of self-worth.

This incredible brain of yours twists the reality of your thoughts, and you feel like you are not good enough or broken, or you start to see the world as a dangerous or threatening place. Well, my friend, this is a cognitive distortion in a nutshell.

WHAT ARE COGNITIVE DISTORTIONS?[4]

What is funny about cognitive distortions is that you don't realize they are manipulating your thinking, and you don't even notice them. You are using them, and you sound rational and accurate to yourself. In other words, you are convinced that the way you think is reality, and it feels true.

The problem with cognitive distortions is that our brains are not all-knowing and do not control reality. So, it is never possible for them to have all the facts. This can lead to some pretty faulty and dangerous assumptions about certain situations. Therefore, it is crucial to stop ourselves from having such harmful thoughts before they proceed to ruin our chances of happiness or, worse, put us in mortal danger. In both cases, they have far too much power over our lives.

This chapter aims to help you recognize these cognitive distortions and teach you how to take your power back. Understanding cognitive distortions is the foundation of Cognitive Behavioral Therapy (CBT), well known as the most effective and standard treatment for anxiety, depression, and other mental health conditions.

Meet Marie. *Marie is in her senior year of high school. She always had a hard time socializing with her classmates, inding herself alone most of the time.*

---

4   APA Dictionary of Psychology. (2022). American Psychological Association. https://dictionary.apa.org/cognitive-distortion

The American Psychological Association describes cognitive distortions as "faulty or inaccurate thinking, perception, or belief." They are often defined by negativity, which is almost always a biased perspective that we unconsciously reinforce over time. All cognitive distortions can be boiled down to tendencies or patterns of thinking or beliefs that are false or inaccurate and can potentially cause psychological damage to the individual.

She is fascinated by fashion design, but is down on herself and shy about liking this, because she thinks it's an unrealistic career goal to have. She hopes that she'll be able to attend college. Because of her family's financial situation, she must take a part-time job that she hates. Marie lives with her mom and two other siblings.
She doesn't have time now for her passion or personal life, and she barely has friends to get out with on the weekend. Now she is on her own, trying to figure out how to succeed in her "unrealistic dream."

We are about to identify the most common cognitive distortions that manipulate Marie's thoughts and make her life a struggle.

All-or-Nothing Thinking. This type of thinking makes you an extremist that can only be on one of two sides, as opposed to being able to see the moral gray area that exists in a lot of situations, as is evident by living your life with an open mind. This makes you think you are either perfect or a failure and have all or nothing. This thinking creates perfectionism and sets unrealistic expectations, resulting in reduced motivation, disappointment, and failure.

Marie, was so upset about her life situation that she thought, *"Why even bother to look into college? I will never be able to afford it."*

She knows this is not a definite reason you can't go to college, but she couldn't see a way out because her income was going toward family expenses. *"I might as well be a waitress my whole life."* So, she gave up on her dream.

Overgeneralization. It comes when you're taking one negative experience and assuming everything will be a disaster. For Marie, she was saying things like: *"I will always have the worst luck in the entire world," "I am the poorest, I will never be a fashion designer,"* or, *"Nobody will ever be able to help me."*

Words like "always" or "never" are used in overgeneralization and make you feel the worst.

Mental Filter. When you take one negative experience and allow it to be the filter by which you view the world – essentially blocking the possibility of seeing anything in a positive light. It's like when Marie lent a friend her Gameboy console, and he misplaced it. Because it was her favorite thing, she vowed: *"I will never give anybody anything."*

There's still some good in the world, my friend. Don't let one negative experience be your yardstick. Not everyone is the same.

Disqualifying the Positive. This type of thinking allows you to see the positive side of things but immediately eliminates them as a possible outcome. When Marie's class-mate Derick offered her his seat on the school bus, she thought,

"There is no way this guy is being nice to me because he likes me; he just wants me to do his homework for him."

Mind Reading. When you wrongfully think you know what somebody is thinking or feeling about you, when you do not, so you jump to conclusions. When Marie had a day off and wanted to hang out with her friend Jane, she was always busy with her extracurriculars. So, Marie would say things like: *"Jane doesn't want to be friends anymore; she thinks I'm terrible." "Nobody wants to hang out with me anymore; they believe I'm a loser."* Mind reading makes you feel fearful, insecure, anxious, or angry, and it is not reason-based thinking.

Unreal-ideal. Social media would be the best example of unreal-ideal thinking. The unfair comparison of ourselves with others always lets us down. It is like being constantly in a competition to be good enough. Marie would compare her life with the social media posts made by all her classmates.

She would think, *"They all have more friends than me." "They are all going to college next year." "They all have money and can afford expensive things and luxurious vacations."* In her distorted thinking, their lives were perfect, and only hers was a mess. She would feel ashamed and discouraged.

Catastrophizing. This is also known as the "what if" question. It happens when you assume that your worries and fears are genuine and you believe that the prediction in your head is the most accurate outcome. When Marie received her scholarship letter from a college because of her high grades, she was happy. Still, she immediately started thinking: *"What if I fail college because I will always be working to support my family and not have time for studies?" "What if I'm stuck in this restaurant for my entire life?"* Catastrophizing makes you feel like everything is hopeless.

Emotional Reasoning. When you feel a certain way and take those feelings as reality, it's like watching your classmates give their presentations and feeling that yours doesn't measure up and never will. Anxious feelings in social situations make you think that you are acting awkward. Marie felt hopeless and worried that she would never go to college to become a fashion designer, so she decided to believe that way.

Labeling. When you pass future and permanent judgment on a person or scenario after one experience. Marie is also a non-confrontational person who tries to keep her dreams and secrets to herself. But one day, she shared with Jane her big dream. Not too long after, she heard from some other classmate that a rumor was being spread about her dream to be a fashion designer.

She feels embarrassed and betrayed, and she vows never to let anybody know about her life, so she ends up ending her friendship with Jane.

"I'm such an idiot; I will never have a friend I can confide in ever again," Marie thought. Even though she is a senior in high school and has her entire life to make new friends, but she has already made a permanent judgment.

Personalization. When you think everything others do is about you, you either believe everything happening is your fault, or you automatically identify as the victim. Taking things too personally will result in feeling overwhelmed, helpless, and guilty, leading to depression and anxiety. Most of the time, we
must realize that it's not all about us. Other people have their own lives to put into order too.

If a customer came in and mistreated Marie, this would make her mad and discouraged, so she would take it personally, thinking, *"What did I ever do to you?"* or *"My boss will think I'm not doing my job well and she will fire me."*

Do you recognize any of these cognitive distortions in yourself?

The truth about cognitive distortions is that they create a reality where change is not possible, making you feel trapped and hopeless when the fact is that with the right help, support, and effort, you can change your thinking and your life for good.

UNDERSTANDING YOUR AUTOMATIC THOUGHTS

Do you ever feel overwhelmed by certain emotions out of nowhere? Do you have feelings that seem out of place for that situation and you don't know what to do?

They puzzle you, making you feel weird inside as you go down this rabbit hole of mistakes, depression, self-deceit, and panic attacks – some more severe than others.

Trust me; you're not alone; we've all been there. At least I have. I mean, I didn't know how to identify the origin of these problems. But I remember when I would ball up in fear whenever I faced a social situation. And now, look at me, I'm helping you.

Showing you the way to learn how to quickly identify your automatic thoughts and get a better hold of them is why I'm here. I have spent years adapting and honing my social skills to control my emotions.

To begin with, I want you to understand what automatic thoughts are.

Our **automatic thoughts** are like pop-up ads, you know? They sneak their way into our brains somehow and cause a sense of discomfort and annoyance. Sometimes we don't even know we're going to a website with so many ads. In the same way, we don't realize we have all these automatic thoughts running through our minds.
That's where most of us stop and go, "Wait, what?"

We try to wipe them off, but they keep coming back as stubborn bugs; they just wait for us to let our guard down. Therefore, we need to know how to identify them. An average of 60,000 ideas and thoughts run through our brains each day, and we really can't think through all of them. So, the brain filters and sends to us repeatedly what it feels is essential and focuses on specific aspects of the situation, giving it a series of plausible meanings. Thus, our thoughts and opinions are born.

They are classified into two types of thinking:

Negative thinking. This sounds pretty self-explanatory, but I guess I'll elaborate for those in the back. Negative thinking happens when your innermost desires overpower and overwhelm your moral compass. If you've seen the cartoon "Luca," you should remember the part where they built their Vespa, and Luca was scared to go on it because of all the negative thoughts and harmful possibili-ties.

Positive thinking. Is finding the root cause of the problem and trying to fix it. It could include a certain level of honesty we are not ready to express. But, hey!

Good things don't come easy. So just like Alberto told Luca, we have to say "Silencio Bruno" to the negative thoughts in our heads and think about the pros and cons of the situation.

Here's another example. So, in schools – pre-school, middle-school, high-school, college, or university – it doesn't matter which one – here's always this kid that gets a 98 on a test and gets angry because he didn't get a 100. The kid is doing great in school, but his insufferable; perfectionist brain won't let him enjoy his success.

To be honest with you, I agree with the guy because, I mean, we all want the best for ourselves. But I draw the line here. Stop trying to cause yourself mental pain and anguish over insignificant details and always trying to be 100 percent perfect. That's how you make yourself depressed for no reason.

It's unnecessary to stress over the fact that you got only 98 on the test and turn it into thoughts such as *"They think I'm not good enough"* or *"I'm meant to get a 100; the teacher must be wrong."* That will only make you more miserable.

Some other kid who got the same scores as the first was over the moon with excitement. His thoughts were, *"Alright, alright, alright! Do you see this score? Do you see it right there on the paper, right next to my name? Don't play with me, mate. I did that!"* And his joy only leads him to study harder next time so he can get those 100 scores and feel even better about himself.

In the next chapter, we will discuss the power of positive thinking, so keep on reading.

FOUR STRATEGIES TO IDENTIFY AUTOMATIC THOUGHTS

James has a lot of friends. He's always calling them, going to their houses or events. He even puts himself in uncomfortable situations just because he believes they will stick their neck out for him, just like he does for them. But lately, James has been very nervous about his final tests. He is looking for someone to partner with and practice, as the situation is getting overwhelming.

Now he needs help, and all those friends are nowhere to be found. Everybody is suddenly so busy and wants him to be there for them, irrespective of his problems. Instead of channeling this into putting himself

first, he had thoughts like, **"Am I the problem? Do they not like me? Have I wronged anybody? Am I a lost cause?"**

He felt anger, sadness, and fear, coupled with his anxiety and depression over the response from his friends, not to mention the tests. Instead of reaching out to them again, James isolated himself, avoiding any contact with them.

This example highlights the negative effect of our automatic thoughts on our emotions and behaviors. If you ever feel overwhelmed, just like James, first things first, you need to take a breather and remove yourself from the situation. Try to look at it from the view of someone outside the situation, or someone else in the scenario. Or talk to your parents and let them help you analyze the situation to find out what went wrong and why you are feeling the way you are. A change of perspective is always best.

Another way is to practice these four strategies of identifying negative thoughts. If this sounds a little bit like therapy, that is because it is.

 *10-minute exercise:*
AUTOMATIC THOUGHTS

1. Write down your automatic negative thought. Be as detailed as possible. Keep this diary or journal and record all the things you have been thinking about recently – school interactions, family situations, friend relationships, etc.

Let's take James as an example; his thoughts were: *"Am I the problem?" "Do they not like me?" "Have I wronged anybody?" "Am I a lost cause?"*

_____
_____
_____

2. Identify their importance. Ask yourself why you think such thoughts and try to find out where they originated. That will let you know why they matter to you so much.

Example: *James couldn't reach his friends and viewed the situation negatively because his friends are important to him.*

_____
_____
_____
_____

3. Think about the best- and worst-case scenarios. Imagine what would happen if that thought were to manifest and become real. Then imagine what would happen if the idea just vanished and never came true. Keep a record of how those two scenarios make you feel.

Example: If James' friends indeed didn't like him, they would avoid helping him on purpose. Let's imagine James diminished his negative thoughts and reached out again to his friends; this time, he got on hold of them, and they practiced for the test together.

_____
_____
_____
_____

4. Retrace your steps. Think back each step of the way to the things that led you to feel this way on such a deep level. You will always find answers at the origin of your thoughts, and once you find that, you can find the strength to conquer them.

Example: James felt anger because his friends didn't reply to him. Sad because he thought that they didn't like him anymore. James was anxious because his beliefs about having no friends and failing his test were too firm. And he got depressed and isolated himself instead of communicating.

_____
_____
_____

This practice is called **metacognition**, where we develop an awareness of our thoughts and begin questioning them. Like all other skills, metacognition can be acquired and harnessed by hard work and consistency, and a tool called the thought record.

WHAT IS THE THOUGHT RECORD?

This involves clarifying and identifying the thoughts that cause problematic emotions. Most of the time, the thought record works best when it is done as soon as those thoughts arrive. Once you have removed yourself from the situation to reduce overwhelming emotions, you can begin the process. Follow these steps each time your brain tries to bring you down.

And to make this more fun, let's make a game out of it. Each time you successfully identify the root of a problem, reward yourself. There are so many ways to do this – you could buy yourself your favorite ice cream, watch a new movie, get a new outfit, or just do one activity that takes you out of your bubble, makes you happy and relaxed, or forces you to interact with others, potentially resulting in new friends.
So, here's how the thought record works:

1. Honestly identify the issue in a situation. To do this, you have to state facts and avoid attaching emotional reasoning to them. For example: "James's friends didn't come through for him when he needed them most because they were busy with their own life problems." As opposed to "James's friends didn't come through for him because he wasn't important enough."

2. Identify negative thoughts and look for positive ways to address them. Make sure to write it down so you don't forget. James felt he was not important enough, and at the same time, questioned if he was worth that importance and how he could make himself essential to them.

Positive thinking would have been to look for someone else, a parent or other trusted adult, to speak to about his current situation, and to find other ways to look out for himself.

3. Identify the emotion you feel. To do this, you must say one word about how you feel. Most of the time, these words are synonymous with anger, fear, sadness, or joy. You can express as many emotions as you want. As for James, he felt anxious, scared, and hurt. This will help you to label your feelings and categorize them while simultaneously releasing their power over you because you are now aware of them.

4. Rate the intensity of the emotion. How deeply you feel about an emotion should tell you how much it's affecting you. For example, James felt at least 40 percent sadness, 40 percent anxiety, and 20 percent anger. With this information, you can deal with the emotions in question in a more successive order going from most painful to least painful and working through them one by one.

5. Retracing your thoughts from the emotions that you feel. For some of you who have trouble remembering what happened that made you feel that way, it helps to consider each emotion you identified as a road that you can work your way through in a backward direction in order to remember what specific thought led to that particular emotion. You can take your time on this. Then you can rate how deeply you believe those thoughts to examine your reasoning further.

6. Create a positive and more adaptive response. This is where you take note of all possible outcomes, find best-case scenarios, counter worst-case scenarios, and come up with some form of "realistic" response to the situation.

These instructions have been made into an easy-to-use table for you to make all your mental discoveries and resolutions, with examples included in bold text:

20-minute exercise:
AUTOMATIC THOUGHTS RECORD TOOL

DATE TIME	TASK	IDENTIFY	RESOLVE
09/07	Identify the issue in a situation.	My mom refused to let me sleep over at my friend's house.	I have identified this as objective truth.
		Your response	Your response
	Identify the automatic negative thoughts and look for positive ways to address them.	My mother hates me, and she never wants me to have any fun. She wants me to be alone all time and do only what she says.	No, that sounds absurd. My friend might not be the best influence on me because he gets in trouble a lot. So, my mom is most likely just trying to keep me away from their influences.
		Your response	Your response

	Identify the emotion you feel.	I feel angry, sad, and peaceful.	I felt angry at first because my mom wouldn't let me do what I wanted. I felt sad because I realized there was nothing I could do about it, but now I feel at peace because I know my mom is trying to protect me.
		Your response	Your response
	Rate the intensity of the emotion.	Before; 80% anger, 20% sadness. Now; 50% peaceful 40% sad 10% anger	My realization of my mother's true intentions has allowed me to properly balance and level out my emotions.
		Your response	Your response
	Retracing your thoughts from the emotions that you feel.	Anger originated when my mother said I was not allowed to go. Sadness originated when I realized my anger wasn't going to fix anything. Peacefulness came when I realized my mother's true intentions.	My emotions were all a result of my state of mind at the time. My thoughts create the emotions I feel. So, if I want to feel good emotions, I need to think positive thoughts.

		Your response	Your response
	Create a positive and more adaptive response.	I will express how I feel to my mother and then tell her that I know she is just trying to protect me, and I will hug her and tell her I love her	This will result in me being a better child to my mother, and it will go a long way in strengthening the good relationship I have with her.
		Your response	Your response

10-minute exercise:
THOUGHT RECORD, PART 2

Select an automatic thought that is most responsible for your emotional distress, and use it to answer the following questions. From the answers to these questions, create a new alternative response to the selected automatic thought you've selected.

Example: Situation: Mom refused to let me sleep over at my friend's house. Automatic thoughts: *"My mother hates me – she never let me have a sleepover."*

1. Do you believe in the effect of the thoughts concerning your situation?

_____

_____

2. Do you have proof supporting this thought?

_____

_____

3. Can you find a piece of evidence against this thought?

_____

_____

4. Can you think of another reason?

_____

_____

5. If there would be a worst-case scenario what would that be? would I survive it?

_____

_____

6. If you would have the best case scenario what would that be?

_____

_____

7. What is the most likely to happen if you get what you want?

_____

_____

8. What if your friend, _____, was in a similar situation, what would you tell them?

_____

_____

9. What actions are you going to take?

_____

_____

ANXIETY

STRESS

FEAR

Solutions

Help

Awareness

Overcome

Discovery

PART 2:

TACKLING SOCIAL ANXIETY

Hey friend, I hope I didn't overwhelm you with all the information and exercises. If I did, take a few minutes to take a breath, OK?

I know this might sound like a lot to handle at once, but relax. There's no hurry to immediately counter or conquer these negative and automatic thoughts and emotions.

We are all people here, and it is only natural for us to want to fast-track things and move on to the next step. But sometimes, we need to slow down. Take a deep breath, and feel deeply grateful for how far we have come. Then take the extra step to analyze our progress as we move through the process. We want to make sure we don't end up making more mistakes, or worse, hurting ourselves deeper than we already have, which will, in turn, hurt the people around us in the process.

Take it easy, friend. Everything will be alright. Trust the process, follow the exercises, and keep reading this book for more answers.

It's better to work slowly and steadily than to rush and fumble. I suggest setting aside time for a 10-minute exercise at the same time every day so you can have a chance to experience the full effects of this workbook.

Finally, after all this effort, please take a moment to leave an Amazon review so that other readers may learn from your experience. Someone's circumstances could be greatly impacted by your feedback. See the QR code page 149.

Thank you for being so supportive!

Chapter 5

CHANGING YOUR THOUGHTS

"Change your thoughts, change your life."

– Jeanette Coron

Identifying negative thoughts is the first step in combating social anxiety.

How to change your thought process in handling certain situations to give you a way to move forward toward a more positive mindset? This process in psychology is called Cognitive Restructuring.

Cognitive Restructuring is about identifying unproductive patterns in thinking about a situation and changing those negative thoughts to more positive ones.

This isn't about forcing yourself to have positive thoughts all of the time and overlooking everything else, no – that's called denial, which can also be a problem.

An example would be thinking of it from the point of how your friend or family members would react to a similar issue. Two main ways to go about this are by positive reframing and examining the evidence.

The aim of this is to consider both the positive and negative aspects of a situation and settle on the process that triggers fewer negative emotions and is a more efficient method to solve the issue.

Positive Reframing. You try to see both sides in unfortunate situations. For example, if you lost your phone, as understandably sad as that is, you could also think of it as a chance to get the new phone you probably had in mind.

Examining the Evidence. This means examining the assumptions you make about how others will react to your situation. You compare it to times when those unfavorable reactions have happened in the past or think of the worst possible trouble that might occur and whether you could handle it if it did.

STEPS FOR COGNITIVE RESTRUCTURING

The following are steps designed to guide you on your journey to restructuring your mindset.

Step 1: Take notes of the situation, thoughts, and feelings.

Pick out a social situation that caused you to have negative thoughts and emotions, and break it into individual parts of negative and positive thoughts. In these situations, the negatives vastly outweigh the positives in number, so pay attention to details.

_____

_____

Step 2: Pick an automatic thought from the list you created – make sure you pick just one thought. Choose the one you've reacted to with the strongest emotions, such as anger, sadness, regret, fear, and disappointment. Now the thought has been isolated, you'll need to transform the thought into a positive statement. You could try something like this:

Automatic thought: *"What if I mess up the science project having to work in the group?"*

Positive statement: *"I can do anything as long as I study hard and practice enough and stay focused on the project not the people in the group."*

_____

_____

Step 3: Look at the situation from different points of view. Mark them down. Then think about it from as many perspectives as possible and discover new thoughts and feelings about that same situation.

_____

_____

Step 4: Craft an alternative response. These questions may have already helped you feel better once you've answered them. But if you want to get the most out of it, try simplifying the answers to the challenging questions into one sentence.

Each sentence will mean a different reaction. You may use these answers anytime the old habitual thinking pops into your head. Allowing the new alternative responses to live alongside the old automatic thoughts might help you feel better and get back on track, even if it's challenging at first.

_____

_____

HOW GRATITUDE AND HAPPINESS AFFECT YOUR THINKING PATTERN

Gratitude is many things to many individuals.

"It involves awe, appreciation, seeing the silver lining in adversity, comprehending plenty, expressing gratitude to God and those in your life, and 'counting blessings.' It is about appreciating the moment, not taking anything for granted, coping, and being present-focused."

According to psychology professor Sonja Lyubomirsky's research, being grateful provides a number of advantages. Those who are appreciative are more likely to be:

- More joyful – helps to maintain healthy relationships and create new ones

- More upbeat – enjoys higher well-being and happiness

- More energized – improves physical and mental health

- More sociable – open to new connections

- More confident – enhances self-esteem in both personal and professional sides of life

Their quality of life is better just from experiencing these feelings more frequently. There are so many ways to show gratitude to ourselves and to other.

Why does gratitude matter to us? Gratitude has a great impact on out lives. As you practice gratitude more, you might find yourself realizing how one positive emotion leads to another or how it balances or calms your negative emotions.

Perhaps you saw how gratitude leads you to positive action or helps build better relationships because it leads to people feeling appreciated for their efforts and for who they are. More positive and grateful emotions bring more possibilities and achievements. I'm about to show you a few fun exercises to practice gratitude.

The Gratitude Jar

A simple and fun daily activity. You need a jar or box, ribbon, markers, stickers, sticky notes, etc. – anything decorative – paper and pen and, of course, consistency.

1.   Find your favorite jar.
2.   Decorate your jar.
3.   Fill up your jar with gratitude.

Every day for at least 10 days consecutively, write down three things you are grateful for that day. Anything is acceptable, such as having lunch with a friend, enjoying your favorite coffee or learning a new skill at school, having a sibling, loving parents or caregivers that are there for you, etc. Let your imagination bloom.

Fill the jar, and every time you feel down, go through your notes and see all the things you are grateful for, and you will realize that your life has meaning and there are so many reasons to feel good about who you are.

The Tree of Gratitude

Here is another way to show gratitude for those of you who are more creative souls and enjoy crafting.

Tools needed: double-sided colored paper sheets, scissors, twigs, string or yarns, tree branches, a vase, and some marbles.

To start this activity, you must gather all the parts for your gratitude tree, find the tree branches, cut the leaves, etc.

1. Find a beautiful vase in your house.
2. Put the tree branches and twigs in the middle.
3. Add the marbles.
4. Make a few leaf cutouts as temples and then transfer them onto colored paper. Cut as many leaves as possible from the start and store them close by.
5. Make sure to punch holes in your leaves.
6. Every day, write down on a leaf one thing you are grateful for – no repetitive stuff.
7. Hang the leaves in your tree. Watch how it grows along with your daily gratitude for life.

Other exercises for gratitude include journaling, prompts, mirror reflection, etc. Practice at least one of them regularly.

Takeaway: When you realize your power over your thoughts, you learn that you have more control over your life than you may have previously realized. Let's look at what else can you do with this newfound power to help you overcome social anxiety. Keep reading to learn about how powerful positive thinking is and how it can help you transform your negative thoughts.

Chapter 6

THE POWER OF POSITIVE THINKING

"Your beliefs become your thoughts, your thoughts become your words, your words become your actions, your actions become your habits, your habits become your values, and your values become your destiny."

– Mahatma Gandhi

Did you ever hear that saying, "Curiosity killed the cat?" Most of the time, social anxiety gets us caught up in trying to either please our peers or not get involved with them when the goal really should be to be a better version of ourselves.

We get so caught up in making ourselves likable that we lose focus on our life plans. We start to see our glass as half empty instead of half full, and before you know it, you're falling into the wrong crowd and doing things your mom wouldn't be proud of in the name of trying to make your glass full.

Some young people, for many different reasons, find themselves attracted to risky behaviors that often end in negative consequences, such as bullying, smoking, drinking, or drug use. Those who don't partake in these activities can get labeled by their riskier peers as stuck up or uncool. Some cave into the peer pressure, and some ignore the negativity and stay committed to their future and their goals.

Do you know what makes this group of people strong? It is that despite the pressure and the natural desire to fit in, they know that where they are headed is better than any of the temptations that provide a temporary fix. And that's the power of positive thinking!

Benefits of positive thinking include:

- Increased life expectancy
- Lower depression rates
- Reduced distress and pain levels
- Increased resilience to sickness
- Improved psychological and physical health
- Better cardiovascular health and a lower chance of mortality from heart disease and stroke
- Reduction in the death rate of terminal diseases.

As a kid, teenager, young adult, or full adult for that matter, it is never easy to steer our minds in the right direction. The "grass is always greener" when we see what other people are doing, but in focusing on other people, we can end up neglecting our own lives.

Life is like a bed of roses. Most people want to see and have pretty roses and forget that the rose plant has thorns.

Positive thinking is about appreciating the beauty of the roses while not forgetting about the thorns. It involves learning to hold the roses so the thorns don't prick you. But just like any learning stage, you may need to fall to get back up. The thorns of life might injure you from time to time, but that shouldn't make you hate life. You just need to stay mindful of the avoidable injuries along the way. The process of choosing whether to pick up a rose or abandon it is determined by your inner dialogue, or self-talk.

As humans, while we e are social beings and are influenced externally by others to some extent, the way we speak to ourselves has a profound impact on how we cope with stress and adversity, the ability to push back against peer pressure, and our overall outlook on life.

We can either push ourselves forward or backward with what we say to ourselves and how deeply we think about it. Large-scale studies divide self-talk into two categories – positive and negative self-talk.

POSITIVE SELF-TALK

Positive self-talk is all about trying to look at things from a more supportive and empathetic perspective. As you might expect, blaming yourself for circumstances beyond your control or seeing a problem in a fixed, catastrophic light can harm your mental health. Therefore, you need positive self-talk to boost your confidence and morale. Positive self-talk includes:

- Daily affirmations
- Acknowledging your progress no matter how small or slow
- Focusing on what you can change, not what you can't
- Focusing on something you enjoy or good memories to take your mind off ruminating about a problem
- Not excessively comparing yourself to others
- Not making excuses.

Daily practice:
MIRROR AFFIRMATIONS

Here's a quick activity to help you practice positive self-talk. Say at least one of the items listed below before you start your day. Look in the mirror and say:

1. "Every day, I am getting closer to achieving my goals."

2. "I am constantly growing and evolving into a better person."

3. "I am fortunate and grateful for everything I have in my life."

4. "I am strong, powerful, confident, and all I need is within me."

5. "My past does not define me; my future drives me. My obstacles can't define me, and I won't let them."

6. "I don't have to be around anyone who makes me uncomfortable."

7. "When I pay attention, I can find things around me that bring me joy."

8. "I am only comparing myself to the person I was yesterday. And as long as the person I am today is even the tiniest bit better than the person I was yesterday, I am already a winner."

9. "Happiness is a choice, and today I choose to be happy."

10. "Today will be a productive day."

NEGATIVE SELF-TALK

Negative self-talk can manifest itself in a variety of ways. It may appear reasonable: *"I'm not good at this, therefore, I shouldn't do it for my safety,"* or simply cruel, *"I'm not good at anything!"*

It may appear to be a reasonable assessment of a circumstance: *"I got a C on the test. I assume I'm not very good at math."* This kind of self-talk can deteriorate into a fear-based fantasy-like, *"I'll never get into a decent college."*

Consequences of negative self-talk may include:

Self-limitations. The more you convince yourself that you can't accomplish something, the more you believe it.

Perfectionism. You start to believe that "excellent" isn't as good as "perfect" and that perfection is possible. In contrast, ordinary high performers out perform their perfectionist counterparts because they are less agitated and more satisfied with a well-done job.

Depressive symptoms. Some studies have found that negative self-talk might exacerbate depression symptoms. If left unchecked, this might have serious consequences.

10-minute exercise:
CHALLENGING NEGATIVE SELF-TALK

After learning how to recognize negative self-talk, it's time to challenge it. What you have to do is to replace every negative thought with a more positive and constructive one. Here are a few examples of how you would reframe your negative thoughts:

Negative self-talk: *No one at my new school likes me.*
Positive reframe: *Wait a second, this statement isn't true. I have my parents who like me and my brother. I even have a new friend that invited me to play video games together. I know there are some people who don't like me but that's OK. I don't have to be liked by everyone.*

Negative self-talk: *Why can't I do a thing the right way?*
Positive reframe: *I know I am really good at doing some things. If I want to get better at something, I can always practice so I can improve.*

Negative self-talk:

_____

_____

Positive reframe:

_____

_____

Negative self-talk:

_____

_____

Positive reframe:

_____

_____

Negative self-talk:

_____

_____

Positive reframe:

_____

_____

Negative self-talk:

_____

_____

Positive reframe:

_____

_____

The Rubber Band

Here is another helpful technique that will bring you awareness when the negative thought needs a replacement. How does this work? When you have negative thoughts or emotions about someone or something, snap the rubber band on your wrist. Take a moment to pro-cess your thought transformation; you can say it out loud, or make a note, or when you gain more experience, make a mental note. Don't let the negativity overwhelm your brain.

Takeaway: The learning process of combating negative thinking is not easy, and it requires lots of practice and dedication. Rest assured, the effort you put in will be rewarding.

Chapter 7

SHOWING YOURSELF SOME LOVE

Have you ever been upset with yourself? Have you ever criticized and shamed yourself for a decision you came to regret? You may have even been too hard on someone, only to be worse on yourself afterward, or you may have put yourself down by comparing yourself to others. Teens with social anxiety tend to compare themselves to others more than those who don't have social anxiety.

Sometimes it might feel like everyone is judging your performance, even if in reality they have no idea what they're doing, and even if you know deep down that your perception is unfounded.

Many people lean toward perfectionist tendencies and self-criticism as a means to achieve their goals. Many believe being hard on oneself is the key to success, especially when juggling school, work, and extracurriculars. You may feel pressured to perform highly in all areas of your life, and it's not always easy. It may take a toll on you over time.

Self-criticism is powerful negative thinking that can lead to severe consequences. It would be best to be gentle with yourself, since harsh self-criticism can lead to low self-esteem, anxiety, and despair. Being critical of one-self is common and usually goes unnoticed. But what if there were another way out?

SELF-COMPASSION

Self-compassion is demonstrated when you forgive yourself, accept your perceived imperfections, and offer yourself love. You cherish who you are. The process of self-compassion is much more complex than it appears, but with the correct guidance and tools, you can learn to make it a habit that persists. These tools include:

Self-kindness. The first step in being kinder to yourself is to be compassionate and understanding when you make mistakes and feel bad about yourself.

Instead of finding so much fault in yourself or severely criticizing yourself while you are already in emotional pain, you should strive to discover the damaging effect of self-judgment and instead treat yourself with care and patience.

Self-kindness can be defined as recognizing your pain and that others face similar or worse challenges. It's about putting things in perspective and recognizing your worth as unconditional, even when you fall short of your expectations, whether in deed or mind.

Some examples of self-kindness include:

- Being kind and compassionate to yourself while you're going through a difficult moment

- Tolerating your own mistakes

- Trying to understand and be patient with yourself when you want to criticize yourself.

Common humanity. It's common to hear the phrase "being a part of something larger," and humans have a natural need to feel connected to others socially. To feel connected to other people, it can help to consider how our own experiences fit into the broader human experience.

Being compassionate with yourself for having limitations demonstrates self-compassion, as does accepting and forgiving yourself for such short-comings. Understanding that all humans have limitations, and that we share common vulnerabilities with others, rather than withdrawing or isolating ourselves when we experience certain emotions, connects us to our humanity.

Examples:

- Recognizing your flaws as inherent characteristics of being human.

- Learning to accept your difficulties as part of life that everyone goes through.

- Reminding yourself that others sometimes feel inadequate, just like you.

Mindfulness. According to the self-compassion theory, mindfulness is the opposite of avoidance since it means observing and labeling your thoughts without having to give in to them.

In other words, self-compassion is when you can recognize negative self-talk or thought distortions without giving these thoughts too much importance. Instead, you would want to find a more neutral place between completely believing your own negative thoughts and completely avoiding them.

Examples:

- Observing your emotions in the face of adversity.

- Keeping things in perspective when you experience setbacks.

- Taking in your feelings with curiosity and openness.

As a result, the self-compassion scale measures this ability. It may also be thought of as a "middle ground" or a method of "balancing" the way you respond emotionally to situations. We will practice mindfulness in the next chapter so you can master it.

FIVE MYTHS ABOUT SELF-COMPASSION

Dr. Kristin Neff has dedicated her career to studying self-compassion. In her book "Self-Compassion: The Proven Power of Being Kind to Yourself," she identifies five myths about self-compassion.

Research demonstrates that the moment we decide to view ourselves with kindness and love, it results in positive emotional well-being. It also helps to avoid harsh self-judgment, anxiety, and depression, and it sparks a happier and more hopeful mindset and approach to life.

The five myths about self-compassion are:

Self-compassion is a form of self-pity. The biggest myth about self-compassion is that it is the same as feeling sorry for yourself. Being compassionate to ourselves is different from self-pity. It helps us recognize negative thoughts and feelings with kindness and empathy.

Self-compassion is a sign of weakness. Remember last time you experienced a challenging situation and didn't use self-compassion? You ended up being frustrated at best, or even felt a sense of hopelessness and de-spair. You were hard on yourself and others rather than having a kind attitude. How we deal with difficult emotions more often than not determines our ability to cope successfully.

Self-compassion means self-satisfaction. Lindsay's dad was always unhappy with his daughter's grades, even though she had difficulty studying due to her health condition. *"You are so stupid! You always embarrass me. You are a failure!"* His verbal abuse was the same harsh criticism he used on himself when facing a problem or a perceived failure.

This was his approach to what he thought was motivating and pushing his daughter to succeed, thinking she was not trying hard enough. Alternatively, he could have been more compassionate to her by saying, *"My dear daughter, I know how hard it is for you to study, but I am here to support you. I love you, and I believe in you."*

Encouraging his daughter with honest recognition and empathy would boost her self-confidence and show her dad's caring support.

Self-compassion is narcissistic. Let's look at the difference between self-compassion and self-esteem.

Knowing that self-esteem is a positive evaluation of self-worth that requires feeling better and above others, it is also a fragile emotion that bounces up and down depending on our success or failure.

Many times, especially in early adolescence, if your self-esteem is hurt, there is a tendency to bully others in order to feel better about yourself.

On the other hand, self-compassion requires awareness and kind acceptance that we humans are not perfect, and mistakes are life lessons. Self-compassion is a more reliable source of support when things don't go the way we want or plan.

Self-compassion is selfish. For years, being modest, empathetic, and caring toward others was viewed as correlating with neglecting or mistreating ourselves. However, the evidence shows that being good to ourselves through self-compassion increases the level of empathy and patience we have for others.

	QUESTIONS	ANSWER
a.	What are the things you mainly criticize and judge yourself for – appearance, relationships with friends, family, or parents, school performance, reaction to a new social setting, behavior in public, etc.?	
b.	Do you use insulting language for self-criticism when any flaws and mistakes are being made, like "I am so stupid," or " I am ugly," or do you use an understanding approach and tone to those like "I'm not perfect, but no one is"?	
c.	What are the feelings you experience when you are being judgemental to yourself?	
d.	Being so hard on yourself makes you more sensitive, depressed, or discouraged. Or does it give your more motivation for self-improvement?	

e.	Does the possibility of accepting yourself as you make you feel scared and insecure, or does it give you hope?	
f.	If you encounter challenges in your life, how do you treat yourself? Are you taking any time to give yourself care and comfort, or are you just focusing on fixing the issue and overcoming the challenge?	
g.	Do you feel out of control of your emotions when angered or saddened by something? Or do you keep calm and observe your emotions with self-compassion as they happen?	
h.	Do you tend to blame yourself for each situation you failed at? Or do you tend to find arguments to reinforce that whatever happened is not your fault?	
i.	Do you tend to enter a negative, self-criticizing state of mind when things don't go as you hoped? Or do you practice self-compassion?	

Most of us are resistant to the idea of self-compassion because of a misinterpretation considering it self-pity. Instead of punishing yourself for perceived wrong thoughts and actions, you can use some empathy and unconditional kindness for yourself while embracing the difficulties of daily life.

HOW TO PRACTICE SELF-COMPASSION

Treat yourself as you'd treat a friend. Consider how you treat people you care about as a good place to start. While we can't make other people's problems disappear, we can acknowledge them and lend a hand to help them through it.

- **Allow yourself to make errors.** The idea that we're all human is the foundation for self-compassion. Everyone else is flawed too, so don't feel bad about it. If a friend didn't answer their phone because they were being lazy, you probably wouldn't immediately label them as someone unpleasant. Allowing yourself to be human is one way to accept your shortcomings and recognize that you're not alone in having them.

- **Care for yourself as you'd treat others.** Connected to the last piece of advice, this one emphasizes being kind and forgiving to oneself. If you realize a friend is sad, injured, or unhappy, you might physically comfort them by patting their back or holding their hand. These gestures, together with accepting, supportive words, can help us experience self-kindness even if we are hesitant at first.

Becoming more self-aware. Practicing self-awareness can be tricky because you must constantly try to reassure yourself that you are enough, even in situations that seem out of control. Some tips on practicing self-awareness include:

- **Make use of "Releasing Statements."** *If you think, "I'm such a bad person for getting upset,"* try *"releasing" yourself from the feeling.* Instead try, *"It's okay that I was upset."*

- **Accepting yourself.** Instead of being dissatisfied or frustrated, try recognizing your character strengths and your perceived areas of weakness as all part of what makes you uniquely you.

- **Engage in mindfulness.** One of the cornerstones of self-compassion is the practice of mindfulness. Many mindfulness-based practices, such as yoga and deep breathing, can be done in even the most unlikely settings. Practicing mindfulness takes you out of worrying about the future or the past, and can help you come back to the here and now.

- **Avoid being too hasty in judging yourself.** Assumptions like, *"I get highly irritable and antisocial on lights"* might be made quickly, preventing you from considering the possibility that your behavior could change. This is just another example of treating yourself with the same kindness and consideration you provide to others in the future.

Get a new perspective. From here, we may need to take some time off to remind ourselves that we are connected to others, and we should shift our attention to reflect that shared humanity is a part of a much larger picture. Here are a few examples of advice:

- **Give up the need for outside approval.** You may punish yourself with negative self-talk for not having the right clothing, or weekend plans, or weight on the scale on considered to be on par with social expectations. It is possible to perceive choosing to put yourself first as an act of self-kindness with a far more significant impact than gaining the approval of people around you who may not even notice the details you are so hard on yourself about.

- **Extending a hand to others.** At first glance, this approach doesn't make sense, but it is about putting your feelings in the right place. When we talk to other people, we find out we're not the only ones with problems. It's a big part of making us feel like we belong, putting our problems in the context of the bigger picture, and building the social networks that are so important to our health.

You learned that mindfulness is a critical component of self-compassion in this chapter. In the upcoming chapter, we'll dive more into mindfulness and how it might help with social anxiety. After learning about positive self-talk in relation to self-compassion, the next question you might have is, "What do I say to myself?" So, here are some ideas for encouraging words:

To increase self-esteem and body image:

- I don't try to imitate anybody because I don't want to be anyone but myself, and I want to improve every day by accepting and embracing my imperfections.

- My weight and the number on the scale has no bearing on my value as a human being.

- My existence and contribution to the world is valuable.

- I have total and unconditional love for myself.

To deal with bullying or social conflict:

- I fit in, and I am enough.

- Nobody can make me feel inferior without my consent.

- Those who treat me nicely are the people I choose to be around.

- I can appreciate the good in others.

- I am safe, and all is well in my life.

- It is okay to say no because those who matter don't mind, and those who mind don't matter.

Takeaway: Self-compassion raises our capacity for generosity, love, and courage. It can make your life and the lives of others better.

Chapter 8

MASTERING MINDFULNESS

"The best way to capture moments is to pay attention. This is how we cultivate mindfulness."

– Jon Kabat-Zinn

Lately, Peace hasn't been feeling like herself. Her younger brother just got a Nintendo Switch for his birthday – something she always wanted that she used to play with her friends at summer camp. For weeks after his birthday, whenever she saw him trying to figure out how to play with the Switch, she would ignore his calls for help and just walk away to avoid him, to the extent that she could not stand being in the same room with him.

She wanted to have her own instead of borrowing from him. She wanted to be friendly and caring, but she just couldn't bring herself to do it. She would get frustrated if he came to her for help or anything else.

After much thought and discussions with her mom, Peace realized she was jealous of her little brother, but felt she should not be. Pessimistic thoughts flooded her head, **"I know I should not be angry or upset. He is my brother, and it's his birthday gift. He'll share if I ask."** Her mom encouraged her to acknowledge her *little brother, let the emotions go, and calmly help him learn the game's rules so they could play it together.*

It's often hard to keep a kind and caring perspective when negative, judgmental thoughts flood your mind.

Mindfulness means, "maintaining a moment-by-moment awareness of our thoughts, feelings, bodily sensations, and the surrounding environment through a gentle, nurturing lens." (The Greater Good Science Center at the University of California, Berkeley)

Accepting that what you feel is valid is a component of mindfulness. When you focus your attention on your thoughts and feelings without passing judgment on them, you'll be able to refrain from thinking that there is a "right" or "wrong" way to think or feel at any particular time.

The purpose of mindfulness is to train your mind to focus on the present, rather than the past or future. How do you do that? Here are a few critical components to practicing mindfulness:

- Notice how you breathe when you feel tense.

- Try to pay close attention to what you're sensing in a given moment.

- Understand that your thoughts and emotions are not constants and do not define who you are.

- Tune into the sensations your body experiences, from how you get comfy in your bed, for example.

- Take pleasure in the small moments of mindfulness you experience throughout the day to help you rest your focus and give a sense of purpose.

I want to introduce you to a couple of mindfulness meditation exercises that will help you tune into yourself. Keep in mind that different types of activities have different ways they'll benefit you. Some research says that mastering mindfulness can be just as effective as cognitive behavioral therapy, but why not try both?

Experiment and see what works for you in getting more comfortable in social situations and trading anxiety and self-doubt for greater self-compassion and well-being.

Mindfulness meditation has the potential to:

- Reduce anxiety, overthinking, and depression.

- Increase self-esteem, self-compassion and general happiness.

- Boost memory retention and learning.

MINDFULNESS MEDITATION PRACTICES

Body Scan Meditation (exercise time 10 minutes, 3 to 6 days a week). This exercise is where you pay attention to different body parts, from your head to your toes. It helps bring awareness to your body when experiencing anxiety or depression, and repeating this exercise will result in more benefits.

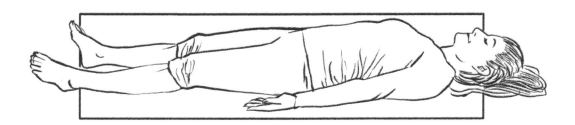

Try this approach:

1. Find a spot to lie, sit, or stand comfortably to relax and practice.

2. Look around the place you are in and slowly transit the attention to your body.

3. With your eyes open or closed, breathe in and out long breaths, and feel your body. Bring awareness that you are here and now.

4. Scan your body starting from your toes, tensing and relaxing them as you go.

5. Feel the sensation of your feet against the floor, the vibration and heat of the weight of your body.

6. Continue by moving your awareness to your ankles, knees, and legs.

7. Move up to your stomach, and feel the vibration of your breathing.

8. Notice your fingers, palms, and arms feel the sensation; are they sweaty, hot, heavy, or aching? Let the tension go.

9. Feel your chest; your heart rate is slow or fast. Breathe in and out slowly.

10. Bring awareness to your neck and jaw, and soften your facial muscles.

11. Be aware of your entire body. Take another breath as you slowly open your eyes, taking in the space you are in and not focusing on anything in particular.

12. Allow your body to loosen up and ease from any tension. Repeat the exercise after a short rest if the results are not yet visible and the anxiety is still present.

The five senses exercise (practice when needed). A simple and flexible exercise to acknowledge your mindful state anywhere you are. The best approach would be if you used all your senses to observe and practice being in the present moment. To do this:

1. Observe **five** items you can see. Look around you and focus on five items you would not ordinarily notice. Pick anything, even a shadow or a tiny concrete crack.

2. Observe **four** things your body can feel. Bring awareness to the feelings you are currently experiencing, such as the smoothness of your hair, the goosebumps you feel from a breeze, the texture of your jeans, etc.

3. Observe **three** things you can hear. Try to become aware of the noises around you. What background noise is there? Is that the sound of a bird chirping, the refrigerator's quiet hum, or the hazy noises of traffic in the background?

4. Observe **two** items you can smell. Please pay attention to scents that you may otherwise ignore, whether good or bad. If you're outside, the air may carry the smell of pine trees or, if you're on the sidewalk, the aroma of a café.

5. Observe **one** thing you can taste. Concentrate on one item you can currently taste. Take a sip of coffee, indulge in some chocolate, eat something, pay attention to the taste on your tongue, or open your lips and sniff the air for flavors.

Walking meditation (10-minute daily exercise). Transform a daily activity into a tool for stress reduction and mindfulness. A consistent practice increases awareness of the feelings our body perceives from the external environment and our internal sensations.

Walking meditation helps us to enjoy the present moment. We tend to notice the surroundings and the things our body senses while focusing on how our body moves. We are no longer on a rushed autopilot that takes us from place to place. You can start with a short walk in a straight line.

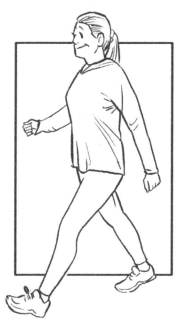

1.   **Find a peaceful place, indoor or out-door, with a short path for 15-20 paces.** Walking meditation's goal is awakening the body and mind rather than reaching a destination.

2.   **Follow the way back and forth, along with becoming aware of your breathing.** Hold a long, deep breath each time you reach the end of the path.

3.   **Pay attention to each movement of your feet.** Notice how high you lift your feet off the ground, the swing of a new step, the bend of your knees, and how they lower back on the ground.

4. Avoid any electronics while practicing. Keep your body straight, your head balanced, shoulders relaxed, hear the sounds from your surroundings, and see the things you usually don't notice. Focus your attention on the present moment.

5. Slow, formal meditation walking might appear strange and awkward at first, but with more practice, it will feel more natural. The results of your mental state after the meditation will be significantly noticeable.

Loving-Kindness Meditation.

"We've been infected with the idea that love is an emotion only felt between two people. But love is universal. It is energy. A contagious force. A gift. To be grateful, to be mindful, to be hopeful and brave, to be forgiving, to be proud is love."

– Jan Lukas

Expressing love and kindness to yourself and the people around you increases happiness and well-being toward yourself, creating strong connections with loved people, strangers, and all living beings.

Loving-kindness meditation requires time and resilience, since it might be difficult and can stir up resistance in some. There are many ways to do this meditation. Here is a straightforward approach:

1. Create a sacred and quiet place where you will be at peace, and set aside the time for yourself. Sit comfortably and close your eyes while relaxing your muscles and breathing deeply a few times.

2. Use your imagination. Try to visualize happiness and wellness. Imagine how it is to feel that you are perfectly healthy and happy. See the love and kindness that embraces you. Breathe all the tension out.

3. Whisper affirmations to yourself such as, "May I be protected and safe!" "May I feel the happiness within me!" "May I be healthy and well!" "May I be appreciated and loved!"

Repeat the affirmations 2 to 3 times or as many times as needed. If you want, you can choose to focus your love and kindness meditation on yourself or on someone in your life. Shift the feeling of gratitude and love to them. Take one person at a time, the closest one to your heart.

As you get to the end of your meditation, open your eyes and remember to revisit all the great feelings you had throughout the process. This might seem like the hardest thing. It involves extending kindness to yourself first, then to someone close to you, then to someone you don't know, and lastly to someone giving you a hard time. By the time you're done, you will have extended kindness to all.

Rating anxiety in the body exercise.
Whether conscious of it or not, our emotions frequently manifest in our mind and the physical body. You can experiment with this technique whenever you feel the onset of worry approaching. Use it for as long as it grounds and nourishes you, exploring it with care and kindness.

Date and Time:	
So far today, have you brought kind awareness to your:	

☐ **Thoughts?**	☐ **Heart?**	☐ **Body?**	☐ **None?**

Bring gentle awareness as to why you were feeling anxiety as you start this meditation.

- When you consider this, pay attention to how your stomach, chest, and head feel and any emotions you may associate with them.

- What impact, if any, has your thinking – positive or negative – had on this bout of anxiety?

- Become aware that many other people have experienced anxiety in similar situations.

- What other feelings or emotions are you experiencing as a result of the issue that triggered your anxiety?

- How can you incorporate the awareness of this meditation into your regular life?

How to practice:

1. You can start the practice in a comfortable sitting position, and you may also think about lying on your back to relax if sitting is difficult for you. In any situation, ensure your eyes are closed, the chest is open, and the spine is straight.

. Watching the progression of five or six breaths can help you ground yourself for a short while.

. Once you've concluded, ask yourself if any emotions are present. Allow your consciousness to be open to anything that could be present rather than actively seeking it.

. If there is an emotion present (such as anger, worry, confusion, sadness, or annoyance), think about where that emotion is located in the physical body. It might manifest as any variety of feelings, including but not restricted to:

• Tightness	• Pressure	• Throbbing
• Heaviness	• Twisting	• Contraction
• Heat	• Coldness	• Lightness
• Tingling		

. Observe this emotion by noticing the feeling or by simply saying the feelings out loud. Acknowledge any instances in which your mind may start to wander from the present moment. When this occurs, return to the bodily sensations you are feeling.

. Spend three to five minutes focusing on this emotion's outward manifestation (or longer if this feels comfortable for you).

. Return to your breath to center yourself when you complete the exercise. Open your eyes gradually when you're ready.

. Sometimes, we may not feel our emotions physically.

. Notice any numbness or complete loss of bodily sensation in this situation. Accept that there are many other ways to perceive your body and its feelings. Remember the importance of breathing in this practice to help you center yourself, and focusing on if a bodily sensation makes you feel uneasy. Explore what it is like to have this physical feeling if you feel it is safe to be present with it. Observe how it changes over time as you pay attention to the experience.

Mindfulness techniques are a great way to help keep you in the present moment when anxious thoughts threaten to derail you. Another great way to stay in the body is through mindful breathing, which we'll explore next in this chapter.

HARNESSING THE POWER OF YOUR BREATH

We often forget to notice our breathing throughout the day, even though it impacts our minds and bodies. Do you catch yourself breathing faster when stressed? Let's read Nadia's story.

September 27 was going to be Nadia's first family Thanksgiving. Her mom had left her home country when she was 18 and pregnant with Nadia, and for a long time, it had just been Nadia and her mom. Now she was going to meet the whole family for the first time in all her 16 years of life. Of course she'd be nervous.

She was bothered for days about what she should wear, how she should eat, the best way to greet her elders, etc. She wanted everything to be perfect so they would like her and accept her as family.

On the morning of the 27th, Nadia was ready by 9 a.m. when it wasn't even a school day. Sitting in front of her mirror, she was going over her lines, trying to find the right words to say. Once the girl heard the doorbell ring, she shrieked. She started pacing and sweating and was experiencing "shallow breathing" as she murmured, "I'm not ready, I'm not ready." When her mom found her, she was close to a full-on panic attack. Nadia's mom rushed to hug her. While holding her close to her chest, they started to count and breathe deeply and slowly until her anxiety faded.

What is shallow breathing? Shallow breathing is a form of hyperventilation where you take in more breaths than usual in a minute. You are not able to breathe normally because you are engaging the diaphragm without your lungs, which contributes to anxiety, an automatic response most people have in stressful situations.

As you already know, your sympathetic nervous system is activated when you are under stress. Stress-related symptoms include quicker or shallow breathing, increased heart rate, irritability, elevated blood pressure, anxiety, and physical tightness or tension. These are components of the fight-flight-freeze reaction.

In the story, it was obvious that Nadia wanted to be part of her new family but was very anxious because she wanted them to love her. With her mother's help, she could get through her panic attack.

Slowing down and taking deep breaths helps you fight the sympathetic nervous system so you can trigger the parasympathetic system, which is responsible for turning off the fight-flight-freeze response.

When you practice deep breathing, your belly becomes soft as you use your diaphragm to inhale deeply to fill the lungs with air. This process lowers your blood pressure, slows your heart rate, and relaxes your muscles. Deep breathing, when practiced, will help you feel better, and your ability to reason returns. Other benefits include:

- Lower blood pressure. Do you really want to have high blood pressure at a young age?

- Improved quality of life, especially for anxious people with asthma

- Improved symptoms of depression and anxiety

- Reduced tension to help with headaches

FOUR BREATHING TECHNIQUES
THAT CAN HELP REDUCE ANXIETY

Belly breathing: When you've been triggered into shallow breathing, you will notice that you can't breathe as deeply as you would if you were conscious of your breathing. To practice belly breathing:

- Place your left hand on your chest and your right hand on your stomach. Imagine your stomach as a balloon that you can inflate and deflate by expanding it (by gently contracting the abdominal muscles).

- Take a steady two deep breaths through your nose. As you breathe in, your stomach will rise. The inhalation should be quite relaxed and mild. Instead of taking a breath in entirely on the first count, picture filling your nostrils slowly as you count from 1 to 2.

- Exhale even more slowly while counting to 3 with no rush. (Pursing your lips might make things easier.) You should feel the stomach inflating like a balloon as you do this. With every little movement, keep your hand on your chest.

- Once you're comfortable with the exercise, increase the inhale time and exhale slowly from 2 and 3 seconds to 3 and 4 seconds to whatever number you're comfortable with.

The humming breath: This relaxation method blends breathing and vibration to relax the body and mind. This practice's pulses serve to rebalance what is hyperactive in the body. Meanwhile, breathing activates the para-sympathetic nervous system and tones the vagus nerve – a nerve that runs from the brain stem to the abdomen. It is one of the main components of the parasympathetic nervous system. It is responsible for the body's "resting and digesting" activities. This practice is excellent for any time of day.

- Get comfortable, and either stand or sit upright.

- Spend at least 5 seconds taking deep breaths through your nose.

- When you run out of air, continue to hum while keeping your mouth shut.

- Repeat between 5 and 7 times.

Pursed lips breathing: When you're struggling to breathe, pursed lips breathing helps to increase the amount of oxygen reaching your lungs, calms you down, and gives you greater control over your breath.

- Take in a breath through your nose.

- Put your lips together and exhale as if trying to extinguish a flame. Make an effort to exhale more slowly than you inhale.

- Repeat five to ten times, pausing if you get dizzy.

Mindful breathing: This is the most basic and straightforward method that develops an awareness of your breath through deep inhaling and exhaling. You might find comfort in a sitting, laying, or standing position, and you may practice this with white noise (a fan, etc.) or calming music.

Performing the 4-7-8 exercise is a beautiful place to start your mindfulness practices regardless of whether you are experiencing anxiety or depression right now.

- Look for a peaceful place.

- Put one hand on your belly above the belly button.

- As you count to 4 and inhale deeply through your nose, you should feel your tummy grow.

- Inhale a deep breath and hold it for 7 seconds.

- Allow your stomach to constrict toward your spine as you exhale for 8 seconds.

Think of where your mind is as you follow the practice. Is your mind here with you at this moment, or is it distracted by automatic thoughts of situations you experienced in the past? What sensations is your body experienc-ing? Bring awareness to your breathing while releasing your thoughts and finding peace in your mind.

Takeaway: This chapter taught us about mastering mindfulness and harnessing our breath. We practiced mindfulness activities and breathing techniques and learned about their benefits. The next chapter brings in another essential social skill for each of us. We'll look at how communication can influence social anxiety and what can be done to take your communication skills to the next level.

Chapter 9

IMPROVING COMMUNICATION

"Communication is a skill you can learn, like riding a bicycle or typing. If you're willing to work at it, you can rapidly improve the quality of every part of your life."

– Brian Tracy

Have you noticed in your relationships with others that:

- When anxious, you tend to pull away from the people you care about?
- You struggle to communicate with words, gestures, facial expressions, etc.?

Having good communication skills lets you build a solid social network, meet new people, and take advantage of life's opportunities.

Socially anxious teens, on the other hand, may feel like they missed out on so much. Anxiety and fear make you want to shut people out, but you shouldn't just accept that.

Having good relationships with others can make your life much less stressful and scary. Having more friends can help protect you from feeling anxious or sad.

Having some social activities in your schedule is linked to better mental health in general. This is especially true if you have social anxiety and want to make friends but are either too scared or don't know how to do so. You may tend to avoid people and social settings because you feel uncomfortable. Still, if you keep running away from your problems, you'll never have the chance to build your confidence and self-esteem or learn how to communicate well.

Jonathan was new to the neighborhood. His family had just moved to Seattle, and he struggled to talk to some of his peers. Most of the time, you would find Jonathan sited on the front porch watching his neighbors play ball in the cul-de-sac, eager to join them but lacking the confidence for it.

He loved to read the encyclopedia and had a passion for dinosaurs. The young man even had clothes and accessories showing different dino species. One could say he's a nerd. He got bullied at his former school because his colleagues believed his love for dinosaurs was childish. Defending his passion, he received snide comments and unnecessary shoves from others.

Now he wasn't sure what to expect from these new neighbors and classmates at school. Rather than putting himself out there to get to know them, he took a much safer approach to his problem. He had concluded that they would also see his love for prehistoric animals as weird, which meant he was strange and would not fit in.

From this example, Jonathan's lack of confidence and experience with healthy friendships made it challenging to handle these situations (like what to wear, what to say, how not to look "weird," etc.). Someone passionate about something could talk with confidence. But that light can be snuffed out by negative criticism.

Grace was one of his neighbors, and she was interested in the "new kid" when he sat on his porch. Grace has always been cheerful and very open to making new friends. Her friends describe her as one who speaks clearly and calmly, maintains good eye contact, listens intently to what others say, and stands up for her friends. She exhibits care and looks for justice in the circumstances.

So when she noticed that Jonathan wanted to come and join them, she went over to meet him and started the conversation. As it would happen, she thought dinosaurs were incredible too. She excitedly introduced him to the rest of the group by being her true 'loud' self, cherishing his passion.

Some people possess the necessary communication skills but lack the confidence to use them in situations they cannot control. Grace, luckily, is not one of those people. Grace is assertive, and is a good example to look to. Practice makes progress, and this book gives you pointers on how to improve your communication skills. With enough exercise, Grace will have nothing on you.

HOW DO I GET STARTED?

- Know the communication areas you would want to work on.

- Identify your trouble spots.

- Learn how to keep the conversation going.

Good communication skills open many doors to obtaining your goals in life. It helps to keep in touch with loved ones and take care of yourself while respecting others. In contrast to popular belief, communication is not a

God-given talent but a skill that can be learned with time and effort. Types of communication skills include:

- Verbal communication

- Nonverbal communication

- Assertiveness

1. VERBAL COMMUNICATION

The truth is that you can acquire skills to enhance your verbal communication. However, some individuals might appear to be masters at it while others struggle constantly. Social anxiety makes initiating and maintaining discussions difficult. Even making small talk might be challenging because it's not always easy to come up with conversation starters.

IDENTIFYING YOUR TROUBLE SPOTS

Have a look at the questions below. This will help you to zero in on what needs improving:

☐ Do I find it hard to strike up conversations?

☐ Do I quickly lose my ability to express myself?

☐ Do I frequently respond to questions with a "yes" or "no" and attempt to keep the
    other person talking so I don't have to?

☐ Do I feel awkward discussing my own experiences?

☐ Do I tend to ramble on excessively when I'm anxious?

You might benefit from the conversational advice provided below if you answered "yes" to at least three of these questions.

Begin the conversation. Do not let your fear of starting a conversation stop you just because no one else is talking.

- Listen carefully to the other person and try to see things from their point of view. You can let the conversation flow naturally as long as you feel at ease talking to this person and safe talking about a subject.

- It's okay to initiate a conversation with someone who doesn't reply since, according to research, strangers in public settings tend to ignore others.

Be polite and respectful.

- Be as pleasant as possible while engaging in a new or existing conversation, which means not talking over someone else while speaking. Wait your turn.

- If you're inside, use your "indoor voice" and try to make your voice louder or softer, depending on the room. In other words, adjust your voice tone depending on where you are.

Be your one true self. We tend to have some small-talk topics in our heads, but don't be afraid to express honest and accurate opinions. Being your true self will result in more genuine discussions.

Avoid overthinking. If you find yourself having thoughts like, *"I don't think they like me,"* or *"I sound so stupid right now,"* try to let them go, tell them *"Out!"* Make sure to process that thought in your mind, then take a deep breath and concentrate your attention on your opponent. Accept the present.

- Accept the experience for what it is, no matter how big or small, and look forward to the next time you can talk to someone. Starting a conversation might seem tough, especially if social anxiety is present. Still, it is the ice breaker in coping with the fear of people.

Where and when can I start a conversation? Identifying a good conversation opportunity is your first step. It can happen anywhere: school, break rooms, stores, streets, events, phone calls, social media, etc., as long as you are willing to put yourself out there and step out of your fear bubble.

Here are some examples of places and conversation starters:

- At the school cafeteria, waiting in the lunch line: *"Hey, I see you got this sandwich. I had never tried it before. How is it?"*

- Your neighbor was waiting for the bus at the bus station when you came: *"Hi, have you been waiting a long time? Usually, it arrives on time, but today is late."*

- You see your classmate at the library working on the project you were both assigned: *"Hi, I see you have started looking up the project material. Can I help?"*

Next, you would want to keep the conversation going and have small talk or continue chatting if it goes well for both people.

Note: Ask "open-ended" questions instead of "yes or no" questions.

For example: *"Did you enjoy the show?"*
Ask instead: *"What did you like about the show?"*

If you notice that the conversation is ending, bring up another topic of discussion.

Suppose there is nothing else to discuss because you are not feeling comfortable or the other person is not showing any interest. In that case, you could be polite and say something like *"Thanks for your time, see you later,"* and walk away.

2. NONVERBAL COMMUNICATION

This refers to the messages you send to others through your posture, body language, and level of interest. Most adolescents with social anxiety may show worry about how they look, making them seem uncomfortable with a "closed off" body language. This implies that how you act tells others what you might feel, and it also means that you might be scared and tense and that you'd be better off alone than in front of other people.

It might be hard to change body positions that feel natural. But changing your body language to look more "open" will send a more inviting message to those around you. With time, open body language will feel more natural to you, and it may even lessen your anxiety.

Here are some "closed" body language cues to be aware of, which you could be doing right now:

- **Slouching**. Think about how you are sitting or standing at the moment. Do you slouch or stand up straight? Are your shoulders relaxed and your arms at your sides, or are you squished up to take up as little space as possible?

- **Looking down.** If you slouch, you probably look down. You might also look down when you walk, meet, or talk to someone. People can tell you're worried or have something to hide when you look down.

- **Fidgeting**. Do you mess up your hair, your pen, or your clothes? If you stop moving around, you'll look less nervous and more sure of yourself. Fidgeting makes it hard for people to pay attention to what you're saying, which is especially important when you're giving a presentation.

- **Putting your arms down.** Crossing your arms in front of you tells people to stay away, whether you do it because you are cold, scared, or just like it. Don't try to do it. If you're cold, put on a sweater.

- **Fake Smiling**. Are your grins sincere? Because with only a slight lip move, your smile might be perceived as fake.

How you can improve your body language and appear more "open" to social interaction:

- **Stand up straight.** If you tend to slouch, picture a marionette with strings going from the top of your head to the ceiling. Let that picture lift your head and pull your body out of its slumped position. Right away, you should feel better.

- **Look someone in the eyes.** If it's hard to look someone in the eyes, look at the space between them. They won't ever know.

- **Smile for real.** When you smile, your upper face also changes. Your eyes get closer together, and you get crow's feet. Think about why you're smiling and if you're thrilled.

- **Move forward one step.** If you want to show interest in a conversation, lean forward, open up, and pay attention. If you're shy, it may be tempting to stay away from people, but this gives the impression that you're not interested or don't care.

- **Slow down and speak clearly.** While you desire to keep the conversation going, your anxiety makes you rush through and end the conversation way earlier than expected. Babbling could show that you are nervous or self-conscious. Slow down so that people can understand what you're saying. This is a way to get people to listen to you.

3. ASSERTIVENESS

Assertive communication represents the honesty in which you express your own needs, wants, and feelings while considering and respecting the needs, wants, and feelings of others. When you confidently talk to someone and keep a non-threatening or non-judgmental manner towards them, you take full responsibility for your actions.

Social anxiety makes it harder to learn to be assertive, especially since sometimes being assertive means not doing things as you usually would. You might find it hard to say what you think and how you feel.

For example, you might be afraid to disagree, always agree with the majority, and never say what you think, making you a passive communicator. On the other hand, you may have changed how you talk to people to control and dominate them.

Ask yourself the questions below to identify where to start your assertive communication practice:

- Is asking for what I want a struggle for me?
- Does stating my opinion make me uncomfortable?
- Is it difficult for me to say no?

If the answer to these questions is a yes, you need the tips below on communicating assertively.

Many people find it challenging to ask for what they want because they feel they don't have the right to or are concerned about the reaction. Think about this – instead of thinking, "What if he says no?" What if you thought, "What if he says yes?" How would that change your desire to ask for something?

You would want to notice and reframe thoughts like, "She could think I'm being impolite by asking," for example. Thoughts like this will only stop you from requesting what you want or need.

When making a request, do the following.

- Sympathize with the other person's situation, e.g., "I know you've been very busy lately."
- Describe your situation and how you feel about it, e.g., "Arts and crafts project is due next Wednesday, and I can't do it alone, and I'm worried I won't get it done right/on time."
- Describe what you would like to happen in as few positive words as possible, e.g., "I'd love it if you could help me figure this out."
- Tell the person what would happen and how you would feel if this request is honored, e.g., "I would help you with the extracurriculars for this week."

Saying no to specific unrealistic requests can also be difficult, but they are pretty necessary. Here are some tips on how to say no and be assertive about it:

- Before you speak, decide what your stand is on the matter. Let's practice saying "NO." Remember a situation when you didn't dare to say "no," such as, "Listen, Lizzy, I would love to spend time with you at the park, but I have a lot of homework to get done today."
- Do not apologize, defend yourself, or make excuses for saying no when it is not necessary. Take care of your own needs.
- For example: If you've been asked multiple times at the restaurant if you want more water and you say "no."

HOW TO BECOME MORE ASSERTIVE

In an assertive statement, the pronoun "I" often appears first. Just because you want to be straightforward doesn't mean you have to be aggressive. Being assertive implies negotiating social situations, so everyone involved comes out ahead, which is different than being aggressive, which pits one person against another.

Here are a few instances of assertiveness statements:

- "I liked chatting with you."
- "I enjoy watching shows together or talking about dinosaurs."
- "I am offended you talked about me behind my back."
- "I get that my younger siblings have greater needs, but it still hurts my feelings that you don't have time for me."

Put these sentences together in an assertive manner:

- Start your sentence with "I."
- Include a verb to express your feelings (like, dislike, want, need, feel, love, hate, wish).
- Additionally, complete the phrase by stating how you feel. Example: "I wish you would understand me, I am feeling very uncomfortable."
- Keep your cool and express your feelings without judging them. It's about coming right out and asking for what you want. As you make it a habit, you'll find that it comes more naturally and easily.

Now that you have learned how to improve your verbal and non-verbal communication, you must continue practicing them daily, including assertiveness.

Avoidance is a common experience for people with social anxiety, as it's often the easiest way to stay out of stressful situations. However, this practice limits you in the long run, and you must take steps to face your fears and step out of the discomfort social anxiety puts you in.

10-minute exercise:
THE POWER OF "I"

Come up with five "I" assertiveness statements other than those listed above.

_____

_____

_____

_____

_____

_____

Takeaway: In this chapter, we highlighted the importance of three forms of communication and how to improve them. Taking small steps to build the courage to initiate a conversation, maintain it, and point out your personal needs is essential in mitigating social anxiety. Assertiveness puts you in the driver's seat and builds confidence.

Chapter 10

FACING YOUR FEARS

"Fear, in evolution, has a special prominence: perhaps more than any other emotion, it is crucial for survival."

– Daniel Goleman, Emotional Intelligence

Another critical step in managing social anxiety is facing feared social situations, crowded places, and dealing with people in general. While this goes against your natural instinct, avoiding these things allows your mind to make them seem even bigger and more scary than they really are.

This chapter discusses the importance of facing fears and provides strategies for how to go about doing this.

Do you often find that:

a. ☐ you avoid making calls or having others call you?

b. ☐ delay in making or answering phone calls?

c. ☐ obsess about what was said during and after calls?

d. ☐ worry about bothering the other person?

Annette doesn't like talking on the phone and prefers texting. She hesitates in making or receiving calls because she experiences severe anxiety and shallow breathing, and her heart races, which is an unpleasant feeling. She's constantly worrying about what she says or how the other person is reacting to what she says.

Sometimes a single phone call might be put off for days or weeks, only for it to take five minutes when you finally get to it. However, Annette avoided calls for the longest time. She would tell people to text her because she felt like it was an environment she could control.

She was 'saving' herself a lot of headaches while acquiring even more headaches. What would she do in her daily life if a phone call was required?

Being frightened by situations that aren't dangerous, such as phone calls or public speaking, can prevent you from enjoying many things. You might struggle with progressing in school, career paths, or even social gatherings and traditions, like having a birthday party or a Thanksgiving dinner with the whole family.

There are several methods for facing your fears head-on. They include:

- Gradually and repeatedly putting yourself in situations that trigger you until you feel less anxious. This is called exposure therapy.

- Evaluate the risk of what you fear by gathering more knowledge on the subject if you're unaware.

- Creating a plan of action for the anxiety-inducing situation, so you feel safer and more prepared.

- Speaking with a professional therapist would be helpful if you're not having much success in facing your fears on your own.

HOW TO PRACTICE EXPOSURE THERAPY

One of the most effective therapies for anxiety or phobias is exposure therapy. It starts with situations that aren't so frightening until you can slowly gain confidence to tackle more stressful situations that eventually become natural and even welcome and pleasant. However, it takes planning and patience.

For example, someone who is scared of people but wants to overcome that fear will:

Make a list. The list would include the situations that you fear.

SITUATIONS I FEAR:

1. Make a phone call in public
2. Do a presentation in front of group
3. Eat in front of others
4. Go to a party and initiate a conversation
5. Visit a crowded aquarium or an exhibit
6. Use the public toilet

Build a fear ladder. Arrange your fearful situations from least frightening to most frightening by rating them on a scale of 1-10. If you have many fears, building multiple lists and ladders is OK, so you don't get confused.

SITUATIONS I FEAR:

☐ Make a phone call in public

☐ Do a presentation in front of a group

☐ Eat in front of others

☐ Go to a party and initiate a conversation

☐ Visit a crowded aquarium or an exhibit

☐ Use the public toilet

Starting with the least fearful goal, list baby steps with which you can achieve the goal. You can include the following list if it will make it easier for you to tackle your goal:

- length of time

- time of day

- environment

- human company.

BABY STEPS TO HELP ME COMPLETE MY GOAL:	
Goal: Prepare for a class presentation	Fear Rating
1. Sit or stand in front of a mirror and talk to yourself, looking into your eyes for a few minutes – Acknowledge your body posture, the tone in your voice, and facial expressions. Feel your emotions.	2/10
2. Imagine that you are now in front of a group. All the eyes are on you, and that makes you uncomfortable. Find a spot to focus your attention. Think of what you have to say, not what you might think others are thinking of you.	2/10
3. Use your phone to record your speech. Listen to it and see where you need to improve.	3/10

4. Ask your parents or any other family member to be your audience, and practice your speech in front of them.	5/10
5. Invite your friend to be part of the audience with your family.	6/10
6. Invite your friends and family to record your presentation, so you can rewatch it and make adjustments.	7/10
7. Present your speech in front of the class at school.	10+

During exposure exercises, it might be helpful to keep note of your degree of fear and aim to stay in specific settings (or keep doing a particular activity) until your fear level decreases by around 50 percent.

Exposure practices require regular repetition, which should help you feel more in control of the situation. With this approach, the fear will lessen faster the more you practice. Remember to periodically go back and re-rate every level of your fear ladder to assess your progress and determine which ones you still need to complete. Reward courageous actions. It's challenging to face anxieties.

Reward brave behavior. It's not easy to face fears. Often, you might get discouraged when you find yourself relapsing or your fears creeping back in. These are the moments to practice mindfulness and self-kindness and to treat yourself when you succeed!

It could be beneficial to use special prizes as a kind of encouragement. For instance, once you achieve a goal, make a plan to treat yourself to something nice. The choice is yours – participate in a fun activity (see a movie, go to a football game, dine out, plan a peaceful night in of a hot bath and read-ing – do your favorite thing).

Use the persuasive power of positive affirmations, such as "I did it!"

COMMON ANXIETY-INDUCING SITUATIONS AND HOW TO HANDLE THEM

Social anxiety triggers vary per person, whether it's handling phone calls, hanging out in small groups, or being the center of attention. They are all valid, and finding the courage to face your fears is one of the few essential steps in overcoming your challenges. Don't get discouraged if things don't work out on the first try – don't give up so easily!

The following list gives some examples of tasks you can use to work your social muscles. Use these to create baby steps to expose yourself to and work on dispelling your fears.

CONVERSATIONAL EXPOSURE FEAR LADDER

When you complete a task, check it off the list and leave a comment on how the experience went.

☐ **Request time from someone.** Ask for the time by approaching someone on the street or in the store.

☐ **Start a conversation.** Talk to people in the elevator or school bus about the weather or a current news story instead of just standing there motionless or staring at your phone.

☐ **Compliment someone.** Offer someone an honest and genuine compliment regarding something you find admirable.

☐ **Speak to a colleague or a classmate.** Try striking up a conversation with a coworker or classmate when you go to work or a class. Inquire about a job or school task or how the weekend went.

☐ **Engage in dialogue.** Try entering a discussion that is already going on at a social gathering, at work, or in class.

☐ **Offer a different viewpoint.** Try expressing your point of view when you disagree with someone's perspective on anything rather than just accepting it out of hand.

☐ **Message a buddy.** Text or make a call to someone you want to get to know better or with someone you haven't spoken in a long time.

☐ **Invite a buddy along for the activity.** Make arrangements for someone to join you for a movie or a walk with your pets.

Add your own ideas below to check off:

☐ _____
☐ _____
☐ _____
☐ _____
☐ _____
☐ _____
☐ _____
☐ _____

THE CENTER OF ATTENTION EXPOSURE FEAR LADDER

When you complete a task, cross or check it off the list and leave a comment on how the experience went.

☐ **Raise your hand and answer that question.** Often, you are too afraid to answer class questions even though you know the correct answer. It's time to break the ice!

☐ **Make a phone call in public and talk loudly**. Avoid hiding in a quiet place to talk over the phone. Do it in front of others and focus on the call, not the people around you.

☐ **Be clumsy and spill your juice at the cafeteria**. Rather than avoiding shaking hands while eating in public, spill the food intentionally. Acknowledge the worst that can happen. It's not as bad as you think.

☐ **Wear a piece of clothing you think is too eye-catching.** If you want to stand out from the crowd, make it bold.

☐ **Give your opinion in a debate.** State what you have to say with confidence and practice what it feels like to be OK with disagreeing with someone.

☐ **Drop your books in the middle of the school hallway or at the library.** Don't worry about making someone momentarily uncomfortable.

☐ **Register for a group sport or band.** Being part of a team requires being the center of attention.

☐ **Participate in a performance.** This exposure will require being in the center of attention and will challenge you in many ways.

Add your own ideas below to check off:

☐ _____

☐ _____

☐ _____

☐ _____

☐ _____

☐ _____

☐ _____

☐ _____

Takeaway: You should have realized already that many teens, just like you, can become more magnified or exaggerated than they need to be, and you might overreact emotionally in some instances. This fear of people that you might experience can be defeated with action and courage. Now you have all the tools necessary for that.

CONCLUSION

It's a lot to take in, practice, and review, but the important thing is that you're one step closer to managing and beating social anxiety. At this point, you should already know the following:

- There is nothing wrong with you. Anxiety is completely normal and has existed for a long time just in a different form as a safety mechanism.

- Anxiety becomes a problem when your body tells you that there's a danger when there's no real danger, and if it starts affecting your daily life and your thoughts, you can work to improve or eliminate the anxiety.

- Symptoms of anxiety are quite similar to shyness, and the root causes as well as the risk factors of anxiety can be linked to various factors.

- Our thoughts, feelings, and behaviors all impact each other, and there are ways to identify and reframe emotions or situations to improve handling social anxiety.

- The power of positive thinking, mastering mindfulness, professing self-kindness, and learning to breathe properly all have a great role in aiding the improvement of anxiety.
  Communication is key.

It is really refreshing to know that you can learn to cope with your anxiety and regain control over your emotions and your life. We can't wait to hear a review from you on how this book helped you overcome your fears. Show your social anxiety that you're the one in control and start changing your life today!

RESOURCES FOR TEENS

Here are some suggestions to keep going beyond the workbook:

APPS

I am: Affirmations tool to remind you how unique you are.

HelloMind: Audio hypnosis to overcome fears.

Mindshift: An excellent app for teens encouraging them to face their anxiety and develop strategies for coping with it.

BOOKS

You can heal your life by Louise Hay

Retrain Your Brain: Cognitive Behavioral Therapy in 7 Weeks. A Workbook for Managing Depression and Anxiety by Seth J. Gillihan Ph.D.

PODCASTS

411 Teen, hosted by Dr. Liz Holfield
The Start of Something, hosted by James Asher
The Youth Mentor Podcast, hosted by Amanda Rootsey

A FREE GIFT FOR OUR READERS

You Get:

☑ **PRINTABLE: Self-Confidence Booster Journal for Teens**

☑ **PRINTABLE: Self-Care Planner for Teens**

Simply scan the QR code or follow the link to gain unique access to these freebies. ***https://bloomingminds.activehosted.com/f/1***

NOTE FROM BLOOMING MINDS

Dear reader,

Your support and feedback mean the world to us.
We sincerely hope that the ***Social Anxiety Workbook for Teens*** has
been a valuable resource for supporting your teen's mental health.

By sharing your experiences in a brief review on **Amazon,** you have the
incredible opportunity to make a significant impact on someone else's life.
Real customer reviews hold immense power in helping prospective
readers like yourself determine the trustworthiness of the content.

Please know that your time and genuine review would be immensely
appreciated. You are an essential part of our community, and your
contribution will help countless others seeking guidance and support.

To post your review, kindly scan the QR code below or follow the provided
link for an easy access. We wish you all the best and urge you to prioritize
your health and well-being.

With heartfelt gratitude,

Your Author!

Leave a Review   **Follow Us**

 Facebook.com/BL00MINGMINDS/

 Twitter.com/_Blooming_Minds

 Instagram.com/social_skills_thrive/

https://geni.us/AmazonBookReviewLink   **www.BloomingMinds.info**

References

Chapter 1

Common Symptoms of SAD. (n.d.-b). D'AMORE Mental Health. Retrieved July 6, 2022, from https://damorementalhealth.com/social-anxiety-self-test/

Social anxiety disorder (social phobia). (n.d.-c). MAYO CLINIC. Retrieved July 9, 2022, from https://www.mayoclinic.org/diseases-conditions/social-anxiety-disorder/symptoms-causes/syc-20353561

Worksheet Bridges to Recovery. (2020, October 10). Causes of Social Anxiety –. Retrieved July 7, 2022,from https://www.bridgestorecovery.com/social-anxiety/causes-social-anxiety/

Center, P. T. (2021, January 15). Social Anxiety in Teens: Signs, Symptoms, and How to Help. Polaris Teen Center: Premier Adolescent Treatment Center in Los Angeles. Retrieved July 8, 2022, from https://polaristeen.com/articles/social-anxiety-in-teens/

Evolve Treatment. (2021, March 31). Social Anxiety Disorder in Teens and Adolescents. Evolve Treatment Centers. Retrieved July 4, 2022, from https://evolvetreatment.com/parent-guides/social-anxiety/

Genetics of Anxiety and Trauma-Related Disorders - PMC. (n.d.). National Library of Medicine. Retrieved July 5, 2022, from https://www.ncbi.nlm.nih.gov/pmc/articles/PMC2760665/

Goldin, P. R., PhD. (2013, October 1). Impact of Cognitive Behavioral Therapy for Social Anxiety Disorder on the Neural Dynamics of Cognitive. JAMA Network. Retrieved July 6, 2021, from https://jamanetwork.com/journals/jamapsychiatry/fullarticle/1727438

Mansson, K. N. T. (2016, February 2). Neuroplasticity in response to cognitive behavior therapy for social anxiety disorder. Nature. Retrieved July 10, 2022, from https://www.nature.com/articles/tp2015218?error=cookies_not_supported&code=8b85d598-39c1-41aa-810b-f353a37373ee

National Social Anxiety Center. (n.d.). FREE SELF-SCORING SOCIAL ANXIETY QUESTIONNAIRE. Retrieved July 9, 2022, from https://nationalsocialanxietycenter.com/liebowitz-sa-scale/

Psycom.net. (n.d.). Social Anxiety Test: 3-Minute Self-Assessment. Retrieved July 6, 2022, from https://www.psycom.net/social-anxiety-test/

Risk Factors for Social Anxiety Disorder | Winchester Hospital. (n.d.). Beth Israel Lahey Health| Winchester Hospital. Retrieved July 3, 2022, from https://www.winchesterhospital.org/health-library/article?id=20196

Screening for Social Anxiety Disorder | Anxiety and Depression Association of America, ADAA. (n.d.). Screening for Social Anxiety Disorder. Retrieved July 5, 2022, from https://adaa.org/screening-social-anxiety-disorder

Social Anxiety Test. (n.d.). Anxiety Treatment Center of Austin. Retrieved July 8, 2022, from https://www.anxietyaustin.com/screenings/social-anxiety-screening/

Sussman, O. (n.d.). Diathesis–Stress Model - Simply Psychology. Simply Pschology. Retrieved July 7, 2022, from https://www.simplypsychology.org/diathesis-stress-model.html

What are Anxiety Disorders? (n.d.). AMERICAN PSYCHIATRIC ASSOCIATION. Retrieved July 6, 2022, from https://psychiatry.org/patients-families/anxiety-disorders/what-are-anxiety-disorders

What Is Social Anxiety Disorder or Social Phobia? (n.d.). What Is Social Anxiety Disorder or Social Phobia? Retrieved July 4, 2022, from https://www.webmd.com/anxiety-panic/guide/mental-health-social-anxiety-disorder

Worksheet 1.1 Pros and Cons of Working on My Social Anxiety - Decision (n.d.-a). Retrieved July 5, 2022, from https://global.oup.com/us/companion.websites/fdscontent/uscompanion/us/pdf/treatments/Mng_Social_Anxiety_wrkshts.pdf

Chapter 2

6 tips for talking to your parents about mental health. (n.d.). ReachOut Australia. Retrieved July 13, 2022, from https://au.reachout.com/articles/6-tips-for-talking-to-your-parents-about-mental-health

Bernett, R. (2020, August 12). Three Reasons Behind Human Stress. Wondrium Daily. Retrieved July 11, 2022, from https://www.wondriumdaily.com/three-reasons-behind-human-stress/#:%7E:text=Animals%20in%20the%20wild%20live,an%20animal%20foraging%20for%20food

Bridges to Recovery. (2019, July 16). How Do I Tell My Family I Have Anxiety and Need Help? 5 Tips for Seeking Support. Retrieved July 14, 2021, from https://www.bridgestorecovery.com/blog/how-do-i-tell-my-family-i-have-anxiety-and-need-help-5-tips-for-seeking-support/

Clear, J. (2020, February 4). The Evolution of Anxiety: Why We Worry and What to Do About It. James Clear. Retrieved July 11, 2022, from https://jamesclear.com/evolution-of-anxiety

Ehmke, R., & Bubrick, J., PhD. (2022, February 3). How to Talk to Your Parents About Getting Help. Child Mind Institute. Retrieved July 12, 2022, from https://childmind.org/article/how-to-talk-to-your-parents-about-getting-help-if-you-think-you-need-it/

The Growth Mindset - What is Growth Mindset - Mindset Works. (n.d.). Mindset Works. https://www.mindsetworks.com/science/

How Cognitive Behavioral Therapy Can Treat Social Anxiety Disorder. (2021, September 1). Verywell Mind. Retrieved July 16, 2022, from https://www.verywellmind.com/how-is-cbt-used-to-treat-sad-3024945

Morin, K. (n.d.). I Had To Find The Root Cause of My Social Anxiety to Finally Heal. Medium. Retrieved July 26, 2022, from https://betterhumans.pub/i-had-to-find-the-root-cause-of-my-social-anxiety-to-finally-heal-307984dde73a

Scott, H. (2021a, January 31). GUIDANCE FOR PARENTS OF TEENAGERS: DOES YOUR SHY TEEN HAVE SOCIAL ANXIETY DISORDER? National Social Anxiety Center. Retrieved July 14, 2022, from https://nationalsocialanxietycenter.com/2018/06/18/guidance-parents-teenagers-shy-teen-social-anxiety-disorder/

What Having a "Growth Mindset" Actually Means. (2022, August 8). Harvard Business Review. Retrieved July 18, 2022, from https://hbr.org/2016/01/what-having-a-growth-mindset-actually-means

What is Anxiety Information Sheet (n.d.). Retrieved July 19, 2022, from https://www.cci.health.wa.gov.au/-/media/CCI/Mental-Health-Professionals/Anxiety/Anxiety---Information-Sheets/Anxiety-Information-Sheet---01---What-is-Anxiety.pdf

Chapter 3

The CBT Model of Emotions. (n.d.). Cognitive Behavioral Therapy Los Angeles. Retrieved July 14, 2022, from https://cogbtherapy.com/cbt-model-of-emotions

Cognitive Behavioral Model (n.d.). Retrieved July 6, 2022, from https://www.therapistaid.com/worksheets/cognitive-behavioral-model.pdf

Monitoring Moods (n.d.). Retrieved July 21, 2022, from https://static1.squarespace.com/static/51e36ea9e4b0e2abc3eb9d10/t/5f07bfeff9b3287d0cf75697/1594343407305/Monitoring+Moods+Sample.pdf

Overcoming Social Anxiety - Larry Cohen handouts(n.d.). Retrieved July 19, 2022, from https://adaa.org/sites/default/files/Overcoming%20Social%20Anxiety%20-%20Larry%20 Cohen%20handouts.pdf

Whalley, M. H. K. (2020, July 5). What is Cognitive Behavioral Therapy (CBT)? Psychology Tools. Retrieved July 16, 2022, from https://www.psychologytools.com/self-help/what-is-cbt/

Chapter 4

Ackerman, C. E., MA. (n.d.-b). Cognitive Distortions: 22 Examples & Worksheets (& PDF). PositivePsychology.Com. Retrieved July 3, 2022, from https://positivepsychology.com/cog-nitive-distortions/

Automatic Thought Record (n.d.-b). Retrieved July 10, 2022, from https://positive.b-cdn.net/ wp-content/uploads/Automatic-Thought-Record.pdf

Casabianca, S. S. (2022, January 11). 15 Cognitive Distortions To Blame for Negative Thinking. Psych Central. Retrieved July 8, 2022, from https://psychcentral.com/lib/cogni-tive-distortions-negative-thinking

How to Reduce Negative Self-Talk for a Better Life. (2022, May 24). Verywell Mind. Re-trieved July 20, 2022, from https://www.verywellmind.com/negative-self-talk-and-how-it-af-fects-us-4161304

Managing Social Anxiety, Workbook: A Cognitive-Behavioral Therapy Approach (2 edn) (2010, May.). Retrieved July 15, 2022, from https://www.oxfordclinicalpsych.com/ view/10.1093/med:psych/9780195336696.001.0001/med-9780195336696-interac-tive-pdf-011.pdf

Positive thinking: Stop negative self-talk to reduce stress. (2022, February 3). Mayo Clinic. Retrieved July 13, 2022, from https://www.mayoclinic.org/healthy-lifestyle/stress-manage-ment/in-depth/positive-thinking/art-20043950

Thought Record 5 Sample (n.d.). Retrieved July 12, 2022, from https://static1.squarespace. com/static/51e36ea9e4b0e2abc3eb9d10/t/5f07c6807594eb11c443609e/1594345089173/ Thought+Record+5+Sample.pdf

UPMC Western Behavioral Health. (2022, April 20). Cognitive Distortions Explained With 10 Examples. UPMC HealthBeat. Retrieved July 25, 2022, from https://share.upmc. com/2021/05/cognitive-distortions/#

Chapter 5

Cognitive Restructuring in CBT. (n.d.-a). Cognitive Behavioral Therapy Los Angeles. Retrieved July 26, 2022, from https://cogbtherapy.com/cognitive-restructuring-in-cbt

Projects at Harvard. (n.d.). Stress & Development Lab. Retrieved July 21, 2022, from https://sdlab.fas.harvard.edu/cognitive-reappraisal/positivereframing-and-examining-evidenc

Suval, L. (2012, August 9). The Relationship Between Happiness and Gratitude. Psych Central. Retrieved July 23, 2022, from https://psychcentral.com/blog/the-relationship-between-happiness-and-gratitude#2

Chapter 6

Affirmations for Teens. (2020, March 8). 7 Mindsets. Retrieved July 25, 2022, from https://7mindsets.com/affirmations-for-students/

K. (2015, December 13). Exercise 2: Self-Compassion Break | Kristin Neff. Self-Compassion. Retrieved July 20, 2022, from https://self-compassion.org/exercise-2-self-compassion-break/

Self-Compassionate Letter (Greater Good in Action). (n.d.-a). Greater Good in Action. Retrieved July 16, 2022, from https://ggia.berkeley.edu/practice/self_compassionate_letter

Chapter 7

Dibdin, E. (2021, July 2). How Meditation Can Help You Manage Social Anxiety. Psych Central. Retrieved July 26, 2022, from https://psychcentral.com/anxiety/how-meditation-can-help-you-manage-social-anxiety#benefits

Fargo, S. (2021a, September 8). Emotional Awareness Meditation. Mindfulness Exercises. Retrieved July 29, 2022, from https://mindfulnessexercises.com/emotional-awareness-meditation/

Mindfulness Definition | What Is Mindfulness. (n.d.-a). Greater Good. Retrieved July 28, 2022, from https://greatergood.berkeley.edu/topic/mindfulness/definition

What is Mindfulness and How Does It Work. (n.d.). Psychology Today. Retrieved July 30, 2022, from https://www.psychologytoday.com/us/blog/theory-knowledge/201502/what-is-mindfulness-and-how-does-it-work

The Five Senses Worksheet (n.d.). Retrieved July 31, 2022, from https://positive.b-cdn.net/wp-content/uploads/The-Five-Senses-Worksheet.pdf

Chapter 8

Three Steps to Deep Breathing (n.d.). Retrieved August 2, 2022, from https://positivepsychology.com/wp-content/uploads/Three-Steps-to-Deep-Breathing.pdf

Upham, B., & Laube, J., MD. (2021, December 13). 6 Possible Health Benefits of Deep Breathing. EverydayHealth.Com. Retrieved August 5, 2022, from https://www.everydayhealth.com/wellness/possible-health-benefits-of-deep-breathing/

Chapter 9

10 Body Language Mistakes You Might Be Making. (2020, December 27). Verywell Mind. Retrieved August 10, 2022, from https://www.verywellmind.com/ten-body-language-mistakes-you-might-be-making-3024852

Adele, T. (2022, June 8). 4 Expert-Backed Breathing Exercises For Anxiety. Forbes Health. Retrieved August 6, 2022, from https://www.forbes.com/health/mind/breathing-exercises-anxiety/

Effective Communication (n.d.-a). Retrieved August 12, 2022, from https://www.anxietycanada.com/sites/default/files/EffectiveCommunication.pdf

How to Have Easier Conversations When You Have Social Anxiety Disorder. (2021, October 21). Verywell Mind. Retrieved August 15, 2022, from https://www.verywellmind.com/talk-people-social-anxiety-disorder-3024390#toc-how-to-talk-to-people

Chapter 10

Effective Communication (n.d.). Retrieved August 20, 2022, from https://www.anxietycanada.com/sites/default/files/Examples_of_Fear_Ladders.pdf

How to Face Your Fears Head On. (2022, February 17). Verywell Mind. Retrieved August 26, 2022, from https://www.verywellmind.com/healthy-ways-to-face-your-fears-4165487

About the Author

Our goal at Blooming Minds is to improve the next generation's life skills by providing access to essential, convenient, high-quality publications that can support them in overcoming any obstacles impacting their mental well-being.

Blooming Minds took the initiative to share knowledge and experience with contemporary research and evidence-based therapies and developed original content to help parents and caregivers raise young adults who are healthy, happy, and confident.

We aim to empower these bright young minds with the resources they require to learn new social skills that will define and shape their prosperous future.

Made in the USA
Coppell, TX
23 November 2024

40868017R00090